SPIRITUAL ESPRESSO
VOLUME 4

By:
Allen Domelle

©Copyright 2019 Allen Domelle Ministries

ISBN: 978-0-9977894-7-8

All Scripture quotations are from the
Authorized King James Bible 1611

Visit our website at:
Oldpathsjournal.com
For more copies write:
Allen Domelle Ministries
PO Box 1595
Bethany, OK 73008
903.746.9632

Table of Contents

JEALOUS FOR BLESSINGS 1
LEARNING THE WORST FROM THE BEST 3
ENDING RIGHT 5
THE GREATEST VICTORY YOU WILL WIN 7
AGGRESSIVE DRIVING 9
THE ROAD OF THE WISE 11
I HAVE OFFENDED 13
VALIANT MEN 15
UNCERTAINTY WITH PEOPLE 17
MULTIGENERATIONAL LEGACY 19
FILLING YOUR HOUSE WITH GOD 21
FORGIVENESS DOESN'T REMOVE CONSEQUENCES 23
"STAND DOWN" CHRISTIAN 25
WHY GOD LEAVES YOU 27
SHOCKED, EMBARRASSED AND ASHAMED 29
UNPLEASANT DUTIES 31
THE POWER OF PRAYER 33
IMPERFECT PERFECTION 35
YOU'RE CONDEMNING YOURSELF 37
GOD'S WORKOUT SESSION 39
WHO'S RIGHT 41
THE MAKINGS OF AN EMPTY LIFE 43
AN APPLE TREE AMONG THE TREES 45
GATEWAYS TO PROTECT 47
FIRST RESPONSE 49
HOLDING GOD'S HAND 51
A PLEASANT BRUISE 53
I WILL GLORY 55
THE IRON FURNACE 57
FRIENDLY FIRE 59
WHERE ARE YOUR PROPHETS? 61

GIVEN TO APPETITE	63
SIN'S LAST WORD	65
FALSE ASSURANCES	67
PARENTING MISTAKES	69
A LOVELY SONG	71
WHEN THE GLORY OF GOD SHINES	73
DANIEL'S STEPS TO PROSPERITY	75
BEFORE THE DEPARTURE	77
THE SILENT KILLER	79
AND GOD SAW THEIR WORKS	81
ARE THOU NOT FROM EVERLASTING	83
SMALL THINGS	85
THE TEST OF TRUTH	87
PRESENTING GIFTS TO GOD	89
AND JESUS WENT ABOUT	91
IMPACTING INTERACTIONS	93
THIS IS JESUS	95
SHINING YOUR LIGHT	97
ONE FLESH	99
FIXING THE BROKEN	101
FOCUS	103
GETTING ALONG WITH OTHERS	105
ENHANCING YOUR LIFE	107
THE GREATEST KINGDOM TO CONQUER	109
FALLEN FROM GRACE	111
STRIVING TOGETHER	113
THE LORD'S MEMORIAL	115
TREATMENT OF THE DISORDERLY	117
PROTECTING YOUR INFLUENCE	119
MISSING OUT ON GOD'S BLESSINGS	121
PROVOKING FAMILY RELATIONSHIPS	123
PLEASANT PLACES	125

THIS IS THE LOVE OF GOD	127
IT ONLY TAKES A FEW	129
THE LORD GOD REIGNETH	131
ACHIEVING SATISFACTION	133
RESPONDING TO TRAGEDY	135
AGE ISN'T EVERYTHING	137
TURNING TRAGEDY INTO TRIUMPH	139
SHIRKING DUTIES	141
SELFISH PARENTING	143
SURROUNDED BY DECEIT	145
DON'T GO TOO FAR	147
REMEMBER THE BONES	149
SALVAGING A PEOPLE	151
PREPARING FOR GOD	153
ALL THESE RULES	155
THE REST PRINCIPLE	157
WHAT DO YOU SEE?	159
ANOTHER	161
IT'S TIME TO MOVE ON	163
DON'T AVOID MERCY AND GRACE	165
WASTING GOD'S POWER	167
BLINDING AFFECTS	169
HARMFUL STUBBORN WAYS	171
WHAT WILL YOU DO WITH FEAR?	173
LESSONS FROM DEFEAT	175
WISHING OR WILLING	177
RESTING IN THE GOODNESS OF GOD	179
DEALING WITH GRIEF IN A POSITIVE MANNER	181
THE WEAKNESS OF STRENGTH	183
A LITTLE TOO LATE	185
ABSALOM'S PLACE	187
THE DOOR OF DEATH	189

WALKING IN INTEGRITY	191
DEALING WITH FALSE WITNESSES	193
MERCY AND GRACE AT WORK	195
SOMETHING'S WRONG	197
LIVING ON YOUR OWN	199
THE END OF THE STORY	201
WISDOM FROM THE SUCCESSFUL	203

Jealous for Blessings

2 Samuel 6:12

"And it was told king David, saying, The LORD hath blessed the house of Obededom, and all that pertaineth unto him, because of the ark of God. So David went and brought up the ark of God from the house of Obededom into the city of David with gladness."

For three months David saw how the LORD blessed Obededom's household because of the presence of the Ark of the Covenant. He originally wanted the ark to reside in the city where he dwelt, but it was placed in the house of Obededom because he moved it in a wrong manner and a man lost his life.

For three months David watched God's blessings on Obededom and those months were difficult because he wanted those blessings on his own life. You could say that David was jealous for God's blessings. It wasn't that he didn't want Obededom to be blessed, but he also wanted those blessings himself. He was happy for Obededom, but it was that he desired those same blessings in his own household.

The desire for God's blessings on your life should be so great that you are jealous for them. Jealousy is not wrong as long as you are jealous for the right reason. Have you seen God's blessings on someone's life and that moved you to be jealous to have the same blessings? Again, it's not that you don't want them to be blessed, it is simply that you want the same blessings on your life. Look at what David did to get those same blessings on his life.

First, David didn't think that he couldn't have the same blessings. When you see someone else whom God is blessing, don't ever think that you can't have those same blessings yourself. God placed that person in your life so you could see them being blessed so that it would whet your appetite to desire the same blessings. God's blessings are for everyone, and He wanted you to see them so you would pursue them.

Second, David acted and did what it took to have the same blessings as Obededom. God doesn't bless someone for no reason. That person did something that caused God to bless them. You must find out what they did and do the same thing. You will find that living in the presence of God will always bring His blessings. The ark was symbolic of God's presence, and David knew if it was in his city that God would bless his household. Living in God's presence always brings His blessings. If you will stay away from sin and serve Him, then you can be assured of His blessings. It is not to say that blessings will come easy, but it is saying that blessings will come if you are willing to put the time, effort and fortitude to get those blessings and endure the hardness necessary to receive them.

Third, David didn't take God's blessings for granted. When God begins to bless you, don't take those blessings for granted. Always remember that those blessings can be taken away as quickly as God gave them. Whatever it took for you to receive the blessings of God, you must continue to do those same things to keep them. When you have God's blessings, be thankful to God that He blessed you. God's grace is the only reason why He blesses you, and you should never take that for granted.

Are you jealous for the blessings of God? Don't just be jealous and do nothing about it, but pursue those blessings on your life. God wants to bless you, but you must be willing to pay the same price that others paid to have them. Let someone else's blessings be the motivating factor in your life to pursue them yourself. My question for you is, are you willing to move beyond being jealous for God's blessings and to pay the price to receive them? If you are, then you will do what it takes to receive them.

Learning the Worst from the Best

2 Samuel 13:6

"So Amnon lay down, and made himself sick: and when the king was come to see him, Amnon said unto the king, I pray thee, let Tamar my sister come, and make me a couple of cakes in my sight, that I may eat at her hand."

The importance of the lessons a person can learn from the story of Amnon could never be over emphasized. Often, when reading this story, we look at Amnon's friend and blame him for the wrong influence he had on his life. This is certainly true. Ammon's friend helped him to come up with a plan to defile his own sister. This was very tragic.

However, I believe we miss one of the most important lessons from this story. Amnon did not learn to be manipulative and deceptive from his friend, but he learned it from his own father. You may recall that David was very manipulative and deceptive when it came to his affair with Bathsheba. What David perceived as a very private act was watched by those closest to him. What David did not expect was that his own children would learn how to manipulate situations to get what they wanted. Amnon learned the worst from the best. He learned how to do wrong from one of the best people in his life.

Several years ago when my daughter was much younger, I learned this lesson as I took her to school. The sun was in my eyes, so I grabbed my sunglasses from the visor. Out of the corner of my eye I saw my daughter grab her sunglasses. I thought I would see if she was copying me or simply trying to get the glare of the sun out of her eyes. I took my sunglasses and put them to my face and then immediately took them away and laid them on my lap. I watched my daughter do the same thing. I did this a couple of times and watched my daughter copy me with every move. That little action reminded me of my influence on my daughter in even the slightest areas of my life.

As a leader, you must be careful that you are not teaching your followers the worst ways of life. You may think that nobody is truly watching you, but your followers see what you are doing and they are copying you. It would be tragic if you teach your followers how to do wrong when on the larger scale you are doing right. What you think is one small indiscretion will be copied by those who follow you. The only difference is they will magnify what you are doing.

Likewise, every parent needs to be very cognizant of the influence they have on their children. The off-color words you use are being copied by your children. The things you watch on TV and see on the internet are being copied. The "little" sins that you are letting go unchanged will be magnified in your children's lives. You must be careful that your children don't learn the worst in life from you.

On the other hand, be careful that you don't use the weaknesses of leaders as your excuse to do wrong. Just because a leader does wrong does not give you a right to do wrong. You are ultimately accountable for your own actions. God does not accept the excuse that you saw your leader do it. God expects you to do right no matter what others may do.

Let me ask you, what are you teaching those who follow you? Are they learning the worst from the best? I challenge you to get rid of those areas of your life that would hurt your followers if they copied them. Don't ever become passive about those areas where you think no one is watching. Always keep in mind that someone is watching you at all times, and your life is a constant lesson from which someone is learning. Be sure they are learning the best from you and not the worst.

Ending Right

1 Kings 7:51

"So was ended all the work that king Solomon made for the house of the LORD. And Solomon brought in the things which David his father had dedicated; even the silver, and the gold, and the vessels, did he put among the treasures of the house of the LORD."

Starting a project is always easier than ending one. You will find that most people can start projects, but very few will follow through to completion. I'm reminded of an unfinished project I would see every time I drove to the western side of Pennsylvania. There was a church that was trying to build a replica of the ark, and for years the steel framework had stayed unchanged and not finished. It became a joke to my daughter and me every time we saw it.

Solomon was a person who not only started projects, but he also finished what he started. The verse above says, *"So was ended all the work that king Solomon made for the house of the LORD."* This project covered several years, but Solomon did not let the longevity of the project stop him from finishing. This project was tedious at times, but he did not let the slow moving intricacies keep him from getting to the end. This project was complex from start to finish, but he did not allow its complexities to bog him down and keep him from getting to the end of the project. He started the project, and he ended it.

One of the areas where your life will be defined is by how many projects you completed. People look at someone who finishes a project with much greater respect than those who never finish what they start. You should never be known as someone who doesn't finish what they start. If you start a project, you must determine to finish it.

One of the things that keeps a person from ending a project is starting too many projects. I've watched many pastors start so many projects that they don't finish any of them. If you are going to be a person who makes it to the end, you must not allow yourself to start so many projects that you can't end them. Only start what you can complete.

Moreover, you must not allow yourself to be sidetracked with what you start. Once you start a project, you must stay focused on it to the end. Don't let yourself become bored with the project to the point that you quit it. It takes character to get to the end of what you start. Everyday cannot be a groundbreaking day. There are some days when you are going to have to plod through to get to the end.

Furthermore, if you are going to end right then you must keep the quality of work all the way through the completion of a project. I have watched many people let up at the end of a project just so they can end it and move on. Don't ever give up quality and effort for the sake of finishing. Do it right all the way through. Give the whole project your best effort, and never let up in the quality of what you are doing.

Let me ask you, do you have projects that are not completed? I challenge you to start taking each project you've started and complete them one by one. Don't become known as someone who can't complete a project. Keep it going and do it right. Be a person who ends right. It will take character and focus to be that type of person, but the effort and character it takes to end a project will help you to have a fulfilled life when you are old.

The Greatest Victory You Will Win

1 Kings 19:3

"And when he saw that, he arose, and went for his life, and came to Beersheba, which belongeth to Judah, and left his servant there."

When you think of great Christians in the Scriptures, Elijah certainly comes to mind. We read the stories of the miracles God performed through him with great delight. These stories motivate us and remind us of the power of God. Certainly, this is what any Christian would want to happen through their life. Yet, Elijah initially lost the greatest battle that he ever fought.

Elijah had a great faith to make it through times of famine, but he initially lost the greatest battle he faced. Elijah's faith was a great faith. When famine hit the land of Israel, God told him to go to the brook Cherith and be fed by ravens. It is amazing that Elijah had the faith to believe that God would send ravens to feed him. God later told him to go to the widow of Zarephath and let her feed him until the famine was over. He had the faith that God could provide through this widow woman with a handful of meal and a little oil in a cruse. Though his faith was great, when he was faced with the greatest battle of his life he initially failed.

Elijah had a great power on his life. When he faced the four hundred prophets of Baal he did not flinch. He understood the power that rested inside him came from God. That is why he was not afraid to challenge Ahab and his four hundred prophets of Baal to a contest. Elijah understood that the prophets of Baal did not have the power to call fire from Heaven. All they could do was put on a show, but when it came time for the evening sacrifice, Elijah put on a show so Israel could see Who was the God. After pouring several barrels of water in a trench and on the altar, he called on God to send fire and consume the altar, and the fire fell. He had the power to ask God to send rain, and the rain fell. Elijah had a great power on his life, but he initially failed when he faced the greatest battle of his life.

What was the great battle he faced? It was the battle over self. Notice the words in 1 Kings 19, *"he saw," "for his life," "requested for himself," "take away my life," "for I"* and *"he looked."* When Elijah came face to face with himself, he failed. He took his eyes off God and placed them on himself, and he failed. He made life about himself and not God. He thought everyone was after him, and he forgot Whom he was serving.

Friend, the greatest victory you will win is the victory over yourself. Life is not about you, but your life is a gift from God to serve Him. When you make everything about you, you will lose the greatest battle. What faith can provide and power can overcome, self will destroy. The greatest battle you will win is when you can crucify the flesh on a daily basis.

Be careful about making everything about you. It is not how others are treating you, but how they are treating God and others. It is not about your legacy; it should be all about Christ. It is not how others perceive you, but what you do to make others see Christ in the right perspective. When you can win the greatest battle in your life, the battle over yourself, then that is when you will see God using your life to influence future generations as Elijah saw when he influenced Elisha. That influence will not happen until you win the battle over self.

Aggressive Driving

2 Kings 4:24

"*Then she saddled an ass, and said to her servant, Drive, and go forward; slack not thy riding for me, except I bid thee.*"

The LORD has blessed me with the opportunity to speak in foreign countries several times. When I go to foreign countries, the one thing that takes getting used to is the way they drive. Their driving is much different from how we drive in the United States.

Several years ago, I took a trip to the Philippines with a pastor friend of mine from the Northwest. It was his first time in the Philippines, and he certainly had never seen driving like theirs. As we sat in the van for about an hour driving to the town where we would preach, the driver was weaving in and out of traffic and passing cars on a curve on a two-lane road. It was no doubt an experience for this pastor. Every time we would pass a car, he held a newspaper up so that he couldn't see the impending danger ahead. In this pastor's opinion, the driver was driving aggressively.

In the verse above, I find that a woman whose son was deathly ill and needed to get to the man of God as quickly as possible asked her driver to drive aggressively by saying, "*Drive and go forward; slack not thy riding for me, except I bid thee.*" This aggressive driving was for the sake of saving her son's life. She knew the only hope for his life was for the man of God to come and touch his body.

Just as this boy needed the driver to be aggressive to save his life, we need Christian's today who are aggressive drivers. No, I'm not talking about going out on the highways today and driving aggressively, but I'm talking about people who need to get an aggressive spiritual drive inside of them. I see too many Christians who have a passive spiritual drive, and it is hurting the lives and souls of those whom they could influence. There are four reasons you need to have an aggressive spiritual drive.

First, lives are at stake. There are souls around you everyday who need to have someone who is aggressive about reaching them before they go to Hell. A passive spiritual drive will only let people go to Hell, but those who have an aggressive spiritual drive will do everything in their power to reach those who are lost for Jesus Christ.

Second, your family is at stake. Today's family is in desperate need for someone to have an aggressive spiritual drive to do right. Families don't accidentally turn out right. They turn out right when someone in the family is aggressive about serving the LORD. The spiritual future of your family will be determined by how aggressive your spiritual drive is.

Third, your future is at stake. You need an aggressive spiritual drive for your own future. Friend, your spiritual future isn't going to be bright if you don't have an aggressive spiritual drive. The drive inside of you to please God should be aggressive. Your future will be determined by your drive.

Fourth, future generations are at stake. You can make a difference in the future if you will step up your spiritual drive. There are generations of people who are not even born who depend on you to do something for God. If you're passive about your spiritual life, then those generations will not see the Christianity you have seen.

Are you an aggressive spiritual driver? Do people see your spiritual drive as different from the rest? I encourage you not to be passive about the things of God. Let your spiritual drive stir you to do more things for God. Don't have the type of drive that just shows up, but have the aggressive type of spiritual drive that is involved, and it involves you with all of your being. This is the type of drive that will make a difference in your world.

The Road of the Wise

Proverbs 1:5

"A wise man will hear, and will increase learning; and a man of understanding shall attain unto wise counsels:"

The road that the wise person travels is always the same. Yes, they may find themselves with different knowledge, but the wisdom gathered was obtained by walking down the same path. Nobody will have godly success without wisdom. Wisdom will keep a person from heartache and will help a person obtain the greatest joy in life.

The Book of Proverbs is a father teaching his son about life. In the Book of Proverbs this father stresses the importance of getting wisdom and understanding. You will find that every person starts out as a simple person, but the choices a person makes at certain junctures of life will determine whether they will become wise or foolish. In the first chapter of Proverbs, the father shows the road a person must take if they want wisdom.

First, if a person wants wisdom then they need to have a heart to receive. Verse 3 says, *"To receive the instruction of wisdom, justice, and judgment, and equity;"* You will never get wisdom if you don't want it. You must have a heart that is willing to receive the instruction needed to obtain wisdom. The person whose heart is hardened towards the instruction of wisdom will find themselves void of it when they need it. If your heart is not tender towards the Word of God and the wisdom It teaches you, you will find foolishness is your future.

Second, if a person wants wisdom then they must have an ear that will hear. It says in the verse above, *"A wise man will hear..."* You cannot get the instruction needed if you are not listening. In other words, you must be more willing to listen than to talk. If you are talking all the time, you will not hear the wisdom needed. Sometimes it is just better to shut up and listen than to put in your two cents. Always be a listener in every spectrum of life in which you find yourself and you will find wisdom is speaking.

Third, if a person wants wisdom then they must have an attitude to learn. The verse above says the wise man will *"increase learning."* Obtaining wisdom is a lifelong class. You must have a desire to increase learning if you want to gain wisdom. In other words, find places where you can learn such as reading books and seeking out wise people who can teach you. A person who is wise is humble enough to understand they have not arrived and will never arrive when it comes to wisdom.

Finally, if a person wants wisdom then they must have a determination to achieve. Attaining unto wise counsels is a determination to achieve. A person who has no desire to achieve will not seek out wisdom. You should have a drive inside of you that desires to be the best at what you do.

You don't have to have a college degree to have wisdom. In fact, I have found that some of the wisest people in life are people who never graduated from college, but they walked down the road of the wise. There is nothing wrong with education, but wisdom is more important. Be sure that every day you walk down the road of the wise so that when you need wisdom to help others you have already obtained it.

I Have Offended

2 Kings 18:14

"And Hezekiah king of Judah sent to the king of Assyria to Lachish, saying, I have offended; return from me: that which thou puttest on me will I bear. And the king of Assyria appointed unto Hezekiah king of Judah three hundred talents of silver and thirty talents of gold."

Hezekiah was a good man and certainly a great king in Israel's history; however, great men can do things that offend others. It doesn't matter how hard you try, you are going to do something that will offend others. The fact that we must deal with other sinful humans tells us that we are not going to always get along with people.

In the verse above, Hezekiah felt that he had offended the king of Assyria. Hezekiah had a tender heart, and he felt that the reason this king sent his army to Judah was because some offense had happened. Though this was not really the case, I find how Hezekiah handled trying to right the offense is a good lesson on what you should do when you have offended someone.

First, take responsibility for what you did. Hezekiah said, *"I have offended."* He didn't get into the finger pointing business with the king of Assyria, but he looked at himself and took complete responsibility for his own actions. The best way you can handle offenses is to look at what you did wrong. Don't be concerned with their actions and what they ought to do, you are the only one you can control. You will never settle an offense between you and someone else until you take full responsibility for what you have done.

Second, get the offense right by restoring what you wronged. Hezekiah tried to pay the king of Assyria back. He thought this would settle the offense. When you have offended someone, apparently they felt that you took something from them or did something to them that was not right. You should do everything in your power to right that wrong. Figure out a way to correct the offense. If you took something you should not have taken, find a way to restore it. If you did something to them that hurt them, find a way to make it right.

Third, don't sacrifice truth to get it right. The one mistake Hezekiah made was that he used the silver and the treasures in the house of the LORD to try and right his wrong. Never sacrifice truth to get something right. Always remember that you don't get right by doing wrong. You get right by doing right. If the only way they feel you can get right with them is by sacrificing truth, then you must always stand with truth.

Fourth, don't expect them to get over it. You find in the story of Hezekiah that the king of Assyria did not accept Hezekiah's attempt to right the offense. Just because you want to get right doesn't mean the other party will accept it. You must accept the fact that they may hold a grudge against you for a long time, and even for the rest of their life. Don't let that stop you from being right towards them. Their actions should not dictate yours. They have to deal with God, and your desire should be to make sure you are right with God and others.

Offenses are going to come in life. These four steps will help you to right the offenses with others, and to also right them in your own heart. You must live with yourself, and if you do what you're supposed to do to get right, then you can have peace in our heart that you have done what is required to get right.

Valiant Men

1 Chronicles 5:18

"The sons of Reuben, and the Gadites, and half the tribe of Manasseh, of valiant men, men able to bear buckler and sword, and to shoot with bow, and skilful in war, were four and forty thousand seven hundred and threescore, that went out to the war."

One of the greatest needs of our day is for men to be men. When I was a boy growing up you didn't have to apologize for being a man. Since those days as a youth, there has been an all-out attack against masculinity. The feminists groups have tried to portray men as sissies, Hollywood has portrayed men as aloof and ignorant and many young men have simply fallen into the mold of what these groups have pushed leading us into a society where it's hard to find real men.

The verse above shows us that there were true men in those days. These men were not just males, but they were men who were valiant. Just because someone is a male does not make them a real man. God shows us several things about these men that made them valiant men.

First, you will notice they were balanced. Notice that they could bear the buckler and sword, but they could also shoot the bow. Other verses show us these men were capable of doing more than one thing. A real man is going to learn to be balanced in life. You may be tough and know how to be an outdoorsman, but you also need to be gentle and know how to care for your children and your wife. Valiant men are balanced individuals who are capable of doing many different things.

Second, these men were willing to fight for right. This is one of the greatest areas in which men lack today. We live in a society where everyone just wants to get along, even to the point that they will sacrifice truth for peace. Men must be willing to stand up and fight for right. Men should not be passive as truth is attacked. Real men don't let their wife handle the tough situations, but they handle the tough situations themselves.

Third, these men were godly. Verse 20 shows us that they called upon God in the battle. True men are involved in serving the LORD. I'm all for a man knowing how to handle himself in the world, but he should also be able to lead spiritually in the home. Being a great outdoorsman may make you a bit rugged, but being godly will make you into a man. Valiant men will know how to handle themselves in worldly affairs, but will also have a close walk with God and will not be afraid to call on Him in times of need.

Fourth, these valiant men were the leaders in their home. Verse 24 says, "...*mighty men of valour, famous men, and heads of the house of their fathers."* Notice, they were the ones in charge of their homes. True men don't make their wife lead in the home; they lead. Let me go a little further and say that true men don't rely on their wife to pay the bills, but they make sure they care for the financial needs of the family.

If there is an area where we need a revival, it is in the area of manhood. Every man should take this devotional and let it motivate them to become a valiant man. Every parent needs to train their boys how to become valiant men. A nation is only as strong as its men. Likewise, a church where men are leading is a strong church, and a home where the man is a true man is a home where there is the security and strength God intended.

Uncertainty with People

1 Chronicles 12:17

"And David went out to meet them, and answered and said unto them, If ye be come peaceably unto me to help me, mine heart shall be knit unto you: but if ye be come to betray me to mine enemies, seeing there is no wrong in mine hands, the God of our fathers look thereon, and rebuke it."

Knowing whether or not to trust someone is certainly a hard thing to figure out. It might be that you have met someone for the first time and you're not sure about them. It could be that you moved to a new area and are not sure whom to trust. It may be that you are attending a new church and are uncertain about the people who attend. It could also be that you just hired someone and are wondering what they will become. The landscape of meeting new people and trusting them may be different, but the uncertainty of trusting them is always the same.

David faced uncertainty about people when he first took leadership in Judah. Saul was dead, and David didn't know whom he could trust. There was a strong following of people who wanted Saul's family to keep the throne, and David didn't know whom he could trust. The men of Benjamin and Judah came to David for they wanted to join up with him in making him king over all Israel. David wasn't sure if he could trust these men, but how he dealt with them is the same way you should deal with people when you are uncertain about them.

First, do not prejudge a person whom you've just met. It is not fair to have your mind made up about someone whom you don't even know. You could be making a wrong judgment about someone who is truly a good person. Give a person a chance to show who they truly are before you make a judgment about them.

Second, let God reveal a person to you. David told these men that God would look on their hearts and rebuke them if they were misleading him. David understood that he didn't know their hearts, but God did. He understood that God had the capability to protect him from those who would try to hurt him if he kept himself right. Likewise, you must trust God to protect you from those who would hurt you. If your heart is right towards God, He will protect you from those who have ill will towards you.

Third, don't open the kingdom until they have proven themselves. David said that he would allow his heart to *"be knit"* unto them if they came peaceably. David wouldn't know whether they came peaceably until some time passed. He was letting time be the justification of whether to open the kingdom to these people. Just because someone may immediately seem trustworthy does not mean they should have the strings of your heart. Everyone should prove the worth of your trust. It is your heart that you must protect. Certainly, you should give them a chance to prove themselves, but you don't have to open the kingdom and let them have full access to your heart. Let time prove a person.

Finally, give others time to trust you. Notice that David said to them, *"Seeing there is no wrong in mine hands."* Not only did these men have to prove to David that they came peaceably, but David had to prove to them that they could trust him. Just because you feel you should be trusted doesn't make it right. Trust is a two-way street. They need time to trust you. Don't get frustrated with them because they don't immediately trust you.

Uncertainty with people is a tool of protection that God gives us to keep us from wrong people. Don't disregard that uncertain feeling in your gut. Listen to it, but don't let that uncertainty make the final judgment. Let time reveal how much trust you should give a person.

Multigenerational Legacy

1 Chronicles 28:8

"Now therefore in the sight of all Israel the congregation of the LORD, and in the audience of our God, keep and seek for all the commandments of the LORD your God: that ye may possess this good land, and leave it for an inheritance for your children after you for ever."

People often talk about the legacy that someone leaves. Presidents desire to leave a legacy that will be remembered. Many pastors have the desire to leave a legacy for which their name will be remembered for generations to come. Many people strive to leave a good legacy.

God showed the children of Israel how they could leave a legacy. Not just a legacy that would last for one or two generations, but a legacy that would last forever. That is an amazing legacy to leave. A person should desire to leave a multigenerational legacy that their family and followers will use for the rest of their lives. Let me show you what it takes to leave a multigenerational legacy.

First, you must keep the commandments of the LORD. It says in the verse above, *"keep...all the commandments of the LORD your God."* God is teaching that we are to keep all the commandments that we do know. We often hear how there is so much of the Scriptures that we don't know, but God is addressing what we do know. You will never leave a multigenerational legacy unless you keep the commandments that you already know. Not just the one's that you want to follow, but all of the commandments.

Second, you must seek the commandments that you don't know so that you can keep them. It is interesting that God said to *"seek for all the commandments of the LORD your God."* This is not what the average Christian would naturally do. God previously tells us to keep what we do know, but seek for those commandments that we don't know. There is a reason God says this. The reason is because it will reveal the heart of a Christian. A person who is seeking to know all of the LORD's commandments is a person who has a heart to please God. This type of person is well on their way to leaving a multigenerational legacy.

Third, pursue what God has called you to do. God told Israel to *"possess"* the land that He had given them. This is doing God's will for your life. You will not leave a multigenerational legacy if you let things sidetrack you from what God placed you on this Earth to do. Find God's will for your life and do it. Don't let petty things, or things that do not pertain to God's will for your life pull you away from His will. Those who leave a multigenerational legacy are those who found God's will and did it their entire life.

Fourth, teach the next generation to keep and seek all of the LORD's commandments and to obey His will for their life. This is the key to the multigenerational legacy. Don't just do these things yourself, but train your children, grandchildren and those whom you lead to do these things. Every Christian should always be training the next generation to do these things.

God promises if we do these things that we will leave a legacy that lives forever. That is a multigenerational legacy. Our homes and churches should have the desire and purpose of leaving a multigenerational legacy. Are you doing your part to leave a multigenerational legacy? If you truly want your life to make an impact, live your life in such a way that you leave a multigenerational legacy.

Filling Your House With God

2 Chronicles 5:13

"It came even to pass, as the trumpeters and singers were as one, to make one sound to be heard in praising and thanking the LORD; and when they lifted up their voice with the trumpets and cymbals and instruments of musick, and praised the LORD, saying, For he is good; for his mercy endureth for ever: that then the house was filled with a cloud, even the house of the LORD;"

"The house was filled with a cloud, even the house of the LORD;" This must have been what David imagined when he initiated the building of the temple. All the work that Solomon and the workers put into the temple paid off when they saw God's presence resting upon it. This was not only a satisfying moment, but it was a sacred moment knowing that God's presence had come down upon the temple.

The temple was called the *"house of the LORD."* I truly believe that our homes should be the house of the LORD. I understand that this was talking about the temple, but wouldn't you want God's presence in your home? If God's presence was in every home, you would find that husbands and wives would get along. You would see brothers and sisters getting along with each other. You would see parents and children working together. If the presence of God was in your home, there is no doubt there would be a different spirit than what you have right now. You can have the presence of God in your home if you will take the steps Solomon took that brought God's presence on the temple.

First, your home must be united in serving the LORD. It is very important that everyone in the home served the LORD together. You must be careful about everyone going their different ways in serving the LORD. Make it a family affair to serve the LORD together.

Second, the whole family needs to make the same sound. You will notice they made one sound. It is important that there are not different sounds coming from your home. What I mean by this is that both parents and children need to be on the same page in serving God. Parents shouldn't have standards and the children look like the world. Husband and wife must be together in what they believe concerning serving the LORD; likewise the children should live the same way as their parents. There should not be two different philosophies of serving the LORD; there should only be one.

Third, the family should praise and thank the LORD together. I believe this is family devotions. You will not have God's presence in your home when you don't have a time when you read the Scriptures and pray together. When the whole family does these things together, you are inviting God's presence into your home.

Fourth, playing the right music in the home is an important part of having God's presence. Music plays an important part in the Christian's life. It would be wise to have good Christian music playing in the background of your home throughout the day. This will help to keep a godly atmosphere in your home.

Fifth, make it a point to talk about the good things God is doing in your home and church. Don't talk about the negative that you see in life, but make your home a place where everyone hears what God is doing in each other's lives. I believe it would be good to have a time of testimony to talk about God working in each person's life. If you made a big decision at the church altar, talk about it with each other. Let the home be a place where talking about God working in each other's life is common place.

You can have God's presence in your home. These five areas are vital to see the presence of God in your home. If God's presence dwells in your home, you will see your family serving the LORD for many years to come.

Forgiveness Doesn't Remove Consequences

2 Chronicles 12:8
"Nevertheless they shall be his servants; that they may know my service, and the service of the kingdoms of the countries."

Rehoboam learned first hand that forgiveness does not remove consequences. In the latter part of his life, he left the LORD and stopped obeying God's commandments. When the prophet came to tell Rehoboam that God was leaving him and going to judge him, he immediately got right. The interesting thing about this story is though God forgave him, the consequences of his actions still had to be paid. Yes, he found God's grace during this time, but forgiveness didn't remove the consequences of what his sin brought.

The forgiveness of God is often misunderstood. There are many who believe that because a person has been forgiven that there should be no consequences. That is completely against Scripture. God forgave Rehoboam, but he still suffered the consequences of his children becoming servants to the king of Egypt.

Let me explain this further. When a person gets saved, their sins are forever paid. They will never have to be concerned with going to Hell. The payment for eternity was settled at Calvary; however, that doesn't mean that God will not correct His children when they do wrong. When they do wrong, God will correct them. Does that mean they are not saved? Not at all! Once a person is saved they will always be saved, but they still must suffer the consequences of their actions. Because a Christian's sins are forgiven does not give them a license to get away with sin, it simply means when they do sin they are forgiven. However, the Christian will still pay the consequence for their sin.

Let me illustrate by using David. David sinned against God by committing adultery with Bathsheba. When approached by Nathan the prophet, David humbled himself and got right with God. God saw this and forgave him; however, David still had to suffer the consequences of his sin. The child that was a result of that affair still died. His family became very dysfunctional because of his sin. God removed the sin from his record, but the consequences still had to be suffered.

This is why we must not let down the standards of the Word of God. There are many well-meaning Christians who think that we need to lighten our standards of the Word of God so we can reach the world. Yet, those standards are not there to make us great Christians, they are there to help keep us from sin. When you lighten up on the standards of the Word of God and tell people that your sins are paid and you never have to worry about paying for those sins again, you are only hurting them. In one sense your sins are paid, but on the other hand you still must pay the consequences for your actions.

Friend, there are always consequences for everything you do. Don't every confuse forgiveness with removal of consequences. Sin always causes a person to lose privileges and freedoms. Sin always takes something from you because there are consequences to sin. Always remember that when you choose to sin, you still must suffer the consequences that sin brings. So, before you choose to sin consider wisely if you truly want to suffer the sin's consequence.

"Stand Down" Christian

Psalm 37:1

"Fret not thyself because of evildoers, neither be thou envious against the workers of iniquity."

"Stand Down," the commanding officer gives the order to the advancing troops. When military troops hear this order they are to stop all military action. There are times when the troops may not understand why the commanding officer gives the "stand down" orders, but they are to obey and trust the commanding officer.

The verse above is a command from God to "stand down." When someone has attacked you and done wrong, it can be easy to launch an offensive against them to reveal what this person has done. God has a reason for the "stand down" orders, and you find what the reason is and what you are supposed to do during the time when you "stand down."

First, don't dwell on what the evildoer has done to you. If you're not careful, you will be consumed with how it seemingly looks that the evildoer is getting away with their wrong actions. God says, *"Fret not...neither be though envious."* The word *"fret"* means to rub away or gnaw at you. It also means to corrode. In other words, if you dwell on how you think the evildoer is getting away with their actions, it will literally cause you to spiritually corrode. It will eat at you and destroy you. Don't be envious or bitter at their actions. You must let it go and move on in life for God promises that their day is coming.

Second, you must trust God that He will take care of the situation. Verse 3 says, *"Trust in the LORD, and do good..."* If you're not careful, you will think that God is not doing anything about the situation. Trust God! God has never lied to you before, and He won't lie to you now. You have to make sure that you do right. God is not going to work on your timetable; He will only work on His timetable. God's timetable is always on time and it is best.

Third, do not take matters into your own hands. Verse 8 says, *"Cease from anger, and forsake wrath…"* If you don't trust God, you will try to help God out and do His work for Him. Christian, that will only make matters worse. You cannot let the works of the evildoer move you to anger and wrath. When they move you to that point, you will try to take matters into your own hands and it will make the situation worse.

Fourth, spend your time doing right. Several times in this Psalm you see God emphasize to the Christian to just do what they are supposed to do. God says, *"Delight thyself in the LORD,"* *"Commit they way unto the LORD,"* *"do good,"* *"Rest in the LORD,"* and *"wait on the LORD."* You must continue doing what you are supposed to do. Keep soul winning and serving the LORD. Keep helping others. Fill your time doing good so that you don't have time to dwell on the bad.

If you will follow these four steps, God will come through. Verse 15 says, *"Their sword shall enter into their own heart, and their bows shall be broken."* If you will continue to do right, God will take the weapons of the evildoer and use them against them. God wants you to let Him take care of them so that your name can be protected. If you take the evildoer out; you will be perceived as the bad person. If God takes the evildoer out, it will be revealed to all who was right.

Friend, "Stand down!" Trust God and don't let the works of evildoers consume you. God will reward them for what they have done, and He will reward you if you do right.

Why God Leaves You

2 Chronicles 32:31

"Howbeit in the business of the ambassadors of the princes of Babylon, who sent unto him to enquire of the wonder that was done in the land, God left him, to try him, that he might know all that was in his heart."

One of the most misunderstood phrases in the Scriptures is found in the verse above when it says, *"God left him, to try him…"* It is misunderstood because God promises that He will never leave us. Yet, in this verse it says that God left Hezekiah.

To understand this verse let me illustrate by using how a dog is trained. One of the commands you teach a dog is to stay. This is an important command for it builds trust between the owner and the dog. When you first start training the dog to stay, you only go a few feet away and see if they hold their position. As your trust in the dog increases, you increase the distance. When your trust in the dog is great, you then leave the dog's sight to see if they will stay. This is all about building the dog's trust in the owner that they will not leave them. They may be out of sight, but they will come back.

This is exactly what God did with Hezekiah. No, God did not leave Hezekiah to never return, but He left him to build him so he could be used in a greater way. The sad part about this test is that Hezekiah failed. He didn't do what he was supposed to do, and because of this he lost God's trust.

Just like God left Hezekiah, there are going to be times when God is going to leave you. There are three reasons God is going to leave you. Your goal ought to be to pass the test so God can use you in a greater fashion.

First, God leaves you because He trusts you. A dog owner will only leave the dog in the stay position for the length of time he trusts his dog to do right. Likewise, God leaves His children at different times because He trusts them. You should not wonder why God leaves you, but you should look at it as an honor that He would trust you to the degree to leave you.

Second, God leaves you to test how much trust He can have in you. A dog owner will only leave the dog at the distance he can trust it. If the owner can't trust the dog out of his sight, he won't leave him out of his sight. God will only leave you to the degree that He can trust you. Your goal should be to let God's trust in you be great enough that He can leave you and not wonder what you are going to do while He is away.

Third, God leaves you so that He can use you in a greater way. The more the dog owner can trust the dog while he is away, the more that dog is useful to the owner. Not only will it be more useful to the owner, but the dog will experience more freedom. God will leave the Christian because He wants to build enough trust so that He can use them more. God only uses a Christian to the degree that He can trust them.

Christian, how much can God trust you? Can God trust you enough that He can leave you, or does He always have to have you at his side? Always remember that you will have more freedom in Christ when He can trust you more. Don't be the type of Christian God can't trust because every time He leaves you mess up. Let God's trust in you be vindicated by doing what you are supposed to do at all times.

Shocked, Embarrassed and Ashamed

Ezra 9:3

"And when I heard this thing, I rent my garment and my mantle, and plucked off the hair of my head and of my beard, and sat down astonied."

Ezra's attitude about sin is refreshing. When he heard that the children of Israel mingled themselves with the people of the land through marriage, it set him back. He didn't go on as if nothing happened, for something had happened. He didn't go on as if he didn't see something, for he did see something. Ezra's attitude when sin came to his attention brought three responses that helped him and the people to overcome their sin. These three responses about sin revealed what was truly in his heart.

First, you will notice he was shocked when he heard about the sin. It says when he heard about the sin that he *"sat down astonied."* The sin of the people shocked him. Though that sin had been around him for years, it still shocked him when he saw it and heard about it.

Too many times we become calloused towards sin. I'm afraid that we are no longer shocked with sin. The first time you saw certain sins it shocked you, but because you have been around it for so long it no longer shocks you. Never lose the shock of sin. Never lose the mentality that it is hard to believe that someone would do that type of sin. This response is very healthy as it encourages a Christian to stay away from sin. When you are no longer shocked with sin, you are more apt to commit the sin yourself.

Second, you will notice he was embarrassed because of the sin. Ezra said in verse 6, *"I am ashamed and blush to lift up my face to thee..."* The embarrassment when he saw it was great. He was so embarrassed with the sin that he blushed when it came into his presence.

When you lose your blush with sin, sin has already began to work on your heart. Do you still blush when you hear or see sin? Do you still blush when you see adultery on the television screen? Do you still blush or feel uncomfortable when you're around the presence of alcohol? You should never become so calloused with sin that you lose your blush. When you lose your blush, you lose your innocency. One of the reasons our nation is morally depraved is because no sin ever embarrasses it. Friend, keep your innocency. Don't every lose your blush when you see or hear of sin.

Third, he was ashamed because of the sin. Not only was Ezra embarrassed when he saw sin, but he was ashamed to even be in its presence. When you sin, are you ashamed? Are you ashamed that you got caught or are you ashamed that you committed the sin? The reason you are ashamed is important. Your response to committing the sin ought to cause you to be ashamed of yourself. If your ashamed because someone caught you, then you are not truly sorry for your sin. A true sorrow of sin will cause a person to be ashamed that they committed that sin.

Your response towards sin is important as to whether or not sin has calloused you. Don't ever lose these three responses when you're in sin's presence. If you lose these responses, sin has already begun to take ahold of your heart. Ask God to help you to never lose these three responses towards sin. Don't let others shame you when you have these responses to sin. These responses will keep you from sin and will help to restore you when you commit sin.

Unpleasant Duties

Nehemiah 3:14

"But the dung gate repaired Malchiah the son of Rechab, the ruler of part of Bethhaccerem; he built it, and set up the doors thereof, the locks thereof, and the bars thereof."

During my high school days I worked at a paper factory. Once a year someone had to go into a tar tank and clean the slag from the walls of the tank and coils. It was one of the most unpleasant duties that most tried to avoid. When I was approached and told that I was chosen to do this job I was not excited about it, but I didn't complain about it either. I took the job and turned what was an unpleasant duty into something that was a challenge to finish in record time. This allowed me to take my mind off the unpleasantries of the job and focus on the job that needed to be done.

Malchiah was the one who was chosen to build a gate by one of the most unpleasant spots in Jerusalem. He was given the task of rebuilding the dung gate. Yes, that is the place where the human wastes would be carried out. It was not a pleasant job. You must realize in those days there was no way to cover the smell. This man took what was unpleasant and completed the job that many would not have done. It was important that he did his job for the enemy would have easily used that portion of the wall to enter if someone wasn't willing to rebuild the wall and the gate by the pile of dung.

Life's duties are not always going to be pleasant. One of the things we must be careful about is that we don't fall into the trap of avoiding the unpleasant things in life. There are unpleasant duties that everyone must do. There are unpleasant duties on the job, in the church, at your home and in life, but they must be done or they will become a place that will harm you in the future.

One of the best ways I have learned to handle unpleasant duties is to get them done right away. At the writing of this devotional, my daughter is going through algebra. Like her dad, she does not like this subject. One day while she was doing her schoolwork I asked her how much more schoolwork she had to do. She told me she was coming down to her last subject, algebra. She said she saved it to last because she didn't like the subject. I told her that the best way to deal with unpleasant subjects is to sandwich them between two enjoyable subjects. I told her to start her day with an easy subject, then take on her algebra, then go back and do a subject she liked. By approaching it this way she could keep her algebra from being that albatross she had to do everyday. Instead of avoiding the unpleasant duties in life, get them done quickly so you can get on to the things you do enjoy.

Furthermore, don't ever think you are beyond unpleasant duties. Malchiah was one of the rulers. Though he was a ruler, he still showed those under him that he wasn't afraid to get his hands dirty. Every leader should show those whom they lead that they are not afraid to do unpleasant jobs. Leaders who won't do the unpleasant duties with their followers are not worthy of leadership. You will gain great respect if you will do the unpleasant duties with those whom you lead.

What are the unpleasantries you avoid? Instead of avoiding them, get them done immediately. Don't put it off, for the longer you put if off the more unpleasant it becomes. If you get them done promptly, you will find that the unpleasant duties won't nag you the whole day and your day will become more pleasant.

The Power of Prayer

Esther 5:1

"Now it came to pass on the third day, that Esther put on her royal apparel, and stood in the inner court of the king's house, over against the king's house: and the king sat upon his royal throne in the royal house, over against the gate of the house."

The Jews faced troubled times. A law was enacted that the Jews in every province over which King Ahasuerus reigned would be killed. Esther had not been called into the presence of the king, and her Uncle Mordecai told her she needed to go at once and show her kindred and what was going to become of them. The problem was that she would be killed if the king did not hold out his golden scepter when she entered his palace. Fasting and prayer was held for Esther, and we see that the power of prayer allowed Esther to be used to save the Jews.

One must never underestimate the power of prayer. Prayer is the one tool every Christian must learn to use daily. If there is anything in Christianity that is not used to its potential it is prayer. We can complain and gripe about what is not going right, but the answer is prayer. Prayer has the power to change many things in one's life.

Prayer has the power to change one's memory. For whatever reason, Ahasuerus had not called Esther into his presence for over a month. Yet, when the Jews prayed, his memory was changed once he saw her. Do you ever wonder if you are forgotten in a ministry? You should pray instead of griping or complaining about leadership forgetting you. Prayer can bring one's mind to remember what they should.

Prayer has the power to change dispositions. Ahasuerus had to accept Esther, and prayer caused him to accept her once he saw her. You may not be accepted in the public arena of your workplace or school, but God can change the dispositions of those around you to accept your stance if you will pray. Maybe your spouse has a bad disposition, then pray and ask God to change their disposition. Maybe your parents or child has a bad disposition, ask God through prayer to make the changes in their disposition.

Prayer has the power to change desires. Prayer caused the king to want what Esther wanted. Prayer changed his desires from having a people killed to protecting them. Friend, prayer has the power to change the desires of anyone. Do you find some areas in your life where your desires are undesirable or wrong? Ask God to change your desires. Prayer has the power to change anyone's desire toward what is right.

Prayer has the power to change history. The prayer of these people literally changed history. The Jews would be extinct had they not prayed. Your prayer life can change history. It can change the history of a wayward child. It can change the history of a troubled marriage. It can change the history of a broken life. It can change the history of troubled finances. It can change the history of a soured name. It can change the history of a dying church. Prayer has the power to change any history.

What do you face today that seems to be unsurmountable? Let me challenge you to let prayer change what you face. There is great power in prayer, but you must pray to realize its power. Don't put prayer off and don't get too busy to pray. You are missing the power that prayer can have in your life by not praying. Let today be the first day of seeing the power of prayer in the rest of your life.

Imperfect Perfection

Job 1:1

"There was a man in the land of Uz, whose name was Job; and that man was perfect and upright, and one that feared God, and eschewed evil."

Every quarter a child gets a report card from their school. On that report card they get their grades recorded for how they did that semester. The goal of each student should be to get straight "A's" on their report card. Just because a student gets straight "A's" on their report card does not mean that they can quit school. Yes, their grades may be perfect, but they still have more to learn. Just because they got straight "A's" does not mean they know everything; rather, it shows they have perfectly learned what they studied, but they still have more to learn.

This is very much the case with what God said about Job in the verse above. God said that Job *"was perfect and upright."* That was quite the glowing report for God to give about him. God was not saying that Job was sinless, but up to this point in his life he was perfect. Up to this point in his life he got straight "A's" on God's report card though he still had more to learn. Though he was perfect he was still imperfect. Though God's report card up to that point in his life was excellent, he still had more to perfect. There are several things we can learn from this statement about Job.

First, as good as you are you still need work. You may be a good Christian, but you still have more areas in your life on which you need to work. Always remember that God's report card is only up to this point in your life. A good report card on your life is not indicative of the future. Likewise, a good report card is only a portion of your life. There are more semesters on which you must be graded. There are more years of your life to be graded before graduating to Heaven. It does not matter how good you are, you still have areas on which you need to work.

Second, being perfect with man is not good enough. God's report of Job was more of a report with man than it was of his whole spiritual life. Friend, you may be able to get along with man, but it is important that your relationship with God gets a good report. Many people are seen as good people in society, but how you are perceived with man is not good enough. How you are perceived with God is what is the most important.

Third, the spiritual is the most important work that one can perfect. Your imperfection with God will eventually be revealed by your imperfection with man. The areas that Job needed to work on with God eventually showed cracks in how imperfect he was with man. Wherever you are weak with God will eventually show up in your relationships with mankind. The one area of your life which you must perfect is the spiritual. Your spiritual side affects all other areas of your life.

Fourth, always remember that the grade on your report card is only indicative of what you have done and not what you're going to do. Always remember that your past does not indicate your future. Yes, it will help you in the future, but there are many who have had great report cards that ended up with a failing grade. Don't get straight "A's" on your report card and then fail in the final years of your life. Don't rely on your past to get a perfect grade today.

Finally, just because you had a failing grade in the past does not mean you can't get an "A" in the end. Don't fall into the trap that you just can't get a good grade in life because of what you have done. Friend, it is not how you start out that matters, but it's how you end. If you have failed in the past, then move on and work at getting a better grade in the future. Let it be said at the end of your life that you got an "A" on your life's report card.

You're Condemning Yourself

Job 15:6

"Thine own mouth condemneth thee, and not I: yea, thine own lips testify against thee."

In an attack against Job, Eliphaz said that Job's own mouth condemned him. Eliphaz was using the words of Job against him in his condemnation. Though Eliphaz and his friends were wrong in their condemnation, he was right in that Job's words condemned him. They condemned him in that he was a good man. They condemned him in that he loved the LORD. They condemned him in that he was filled with pride. Job's words condemned him in both a good and a bad way.

If you listen to a person long enough, you will always find out who they truly are and what they believe. Every person always says enough to condemn themselves. They may condemn themselves in a good way or they may condemn themselves in a bad way. Let me give you some cautions about the words you say.

First, be slow to speak. Quick answers get many people in trouble. Quick answers don't always reveal your true heart, they simply reveal what you feel in the heat of the moment. You would be wise to slow down and think before you say anything. Don't be a person who is always having to apologize for saying something in the heat of the moment.

Second, speak as though someone is always listening. One of the mistakes many people make is that they say something privately thinking that nobody will hear, but you never know who is around the corner or who is recording what you say. You must always speak as if you are being recorded and that it may be used against you in the future. If you would not want someone to hear what you say, then don't say it for they will probably find out. Always remember that as soon as words come from your lips they will be heard and used against you for good or bad.

Third, don't speak lies. The problem with telling lies is that you must remember which lie you told and to whom you told it. The best thing you could do is to tell the truth at all times. Tell the truth because it is the right thing to do, but also tell the truth because your memory is not good enough to remember your lies.

Fourth, be careful with what you write. Many people get themselves in trouble by writing something they wish they had never written. I've always told people what you write is forever inscribed and will be used against you. Be careful what you write or post on your social networking sites. Be careful with what you text, for you might accidentally text it to the wrong person. The best rule to live by is to only write what you want everyone to read.

Fifth, keep a pure heart and you will speak the right things. The best way to keep your words right is to keep your heart right. If your heart is right, your words will be right. You may be able to protect what you say if your heart is not right, but eventually what is in your heart will leak out into words. Keep right with God and your words will be wholesome words.

What have you said lately that will be used against you? Would you want everything you have said in the past month to be broadcasted to everyone? Let what you say condemn you for good. Always keep in mind that every word you write or say will be used against you. Don't let your words condemn you for wrong; instead, let them condemn you for good.

God's Workout Session

Job 23:6

"Will he plead against me with his great power? No; but he would put strength in me."

Job had a false view of how God strengthens His children. Job believed that God would strengthen him without struggle. He didn't think that what he was going through was God's way of strengthening him, but it was. When Job's trials were over he was a much stronger person spiritually than he was when he began.

The Christian must realize that God's workout session is not going to be easy. When a person desires to gain strength, they don't ask to lift light weights. They add weight to the barbell and struggle with it, but that struggle gives them more strength. Likewise, God must send His children through His workout session of struggle so they can become stronger.

Look at the Apostle Paul. Paul struggled with some sort of eye disease. Three times the Apostle Paul asked God to remove the disease, but God told him in 2 Corinthians 12:9, *"And he said unto me, My grace is sufficient for thee: for my strength is made perfect in weakness. Most gladly therefore will I rather glory in my infirmities, that the power of Christ may rest upon me."* No, God did not remove the trial from Paul's life, but He gave him the grace to lift that trial which resulted in him becoming a stronger Christian.

The burdens and heartaches God places upon you are there to help you become a stronger Christian. The struggles that God allows you to go through put you under pressure, but the pressure strengthens you as a Christian. It strengthens you because you run to God for help through prayer. Prayer always strengthens the Christian. It strengthens you because you learn how to lift that weight which will help you to help others when they lift the same trial. When you look at every heartache you face, know that it was given to you to strengthen you.

You can do one of two things when you are placed in God's workout session. You can continue to go on and let it strengthen you, or you can quit and never realize the strength God had planned for you. God placed you under the burden of your trials because He knew it would make you stronger. Is it pleasant to go through God's workout session. Not at all! But, it will help you to be a stronger Christian once you've gone through it.

Furthermore, always remember that God will never place more on you than you can bear. 1 Corinthians 10:13 reminds us, *"There hath no temptation taken you but such as is common to man: but God is faithful, who will not suffer you to be tempted above that ye are able; but will with the temptation also make a way to escape, that ye may be able to bear it."* You can always be assured that if God approved the trial you face then He knew you could take it.

Friend, no one may understand what you are facing today, but you can be assured that God is in control. He simply placed you in His workout session to strengthen you so that you can be used in a greater way. Don't fight it; lift it. Let the grace of God help you as you endure your trial, for when the trial is complete you will find yourself a stronger Christian. If you give up, you will never realize the strength God had intended for you. Keep lifting the weight God has placed you under, for that weight is simply God's workout session to strengthen you for even greater opportunities.

Who's Right

Job 32:2

"Then was kindled the wrath of Elihu the son of Barachel the Buzite, of the kindred of Ram: against Job was his wrath kindled, because he justified himself rather than God."

Recently, I was witnessing to an individual who asked me several questions about the Scriptures. This person told me they watched a television program that had said Adam and Eve were not really created. My response to this individual was that if I had to choose to trust man or God, I would choose God every time.

That is what Elihu was saying in the verse above. He was upset at Job for justifying himself instead of justifying what God was doing to Him. Elihu heard Job say how the Almighty was hurting him, and never one time said that God had a right to do to him what He wanted.

If you must choose between a man and God, you should always choose God. I know this sounds elementary, but too many people in Christianity are choosing man over God. It doesn't matter what the Scriptures teach, if a man says to do something different many will follow what the man has taught. This is absurd and wrong.

Leadership must be careful to always choose God over their staff. Pastors must be careful that they don't choose to defend their staff when their staff has done something wrong. I certainly understand the philosophy of defending your staff, but if they are wrong you must choose God. Don't fall into the trap of justifying your staff over God's Word. You may think this never happens, but I see it happen time and time again to the detriment of leadership's credibility. Leadership on all levels must justify God's commandments over man's sins.

Followers must be careful about choosing God over an admired leader. There is nothing wrong with being loyal to your leader, but blindly following them into doctrinal error or covering sin is not right. When a leader commits a sin, you must not justify their sin. When a leader teaches something contrary to the Word of God, don't justify man by using the age-old argument that it is all semantics. Semantics has nothing to do with right and wrong. If error is taught by a leader, you always justify God's Word by standing behind what His Word teaches.

Friends must be careful about choosing a friend over God. Again, when a friend of a lifetime has done wrong, you must always obey God's Word. Luke 14:26 says, *"If any man come to me, and hate not his father, and mother, and wife, and children, and brethren, and sisters, yea, and his own life also, he cannot be my disciple."* God is teaching that your love for family and friends must never override your love for God and obedience to His Word. Yes, they will tell you at times you hate them, but you must never choose to defend the wrong of a friend.

The Scriptures teach in Romans 3:4, *"...let God be true, but every man a liar..."* Whenever you are faced with who is right, always *"let God be true."* Don't fall into the trap of justifying wrong to defend your situation or the situation of someone you admire or love. Truth must always be what you choose to defend and stand behind. This may be tough, but tough love is what helps those who are wrong to see the error of their ways.

The Makings of an Empty Life

Ecclesiastes 2:18

"Yea, I hated all my labour which I had taken under the sun: because I should leave it unto the man that shall be after me."

When you look at the life of Solomon, you would think that when he got old he would have looked back and saw a full life of blessings. Yet, when you read Ecclesiastes 2, you see a man whose life was empty. Here was a man who grew up in the household of David, the greatest king in Isreal's history. He grew up in a house where he saw God's blessings on his father's life firsthand. In the early years of his reign, he personally experienced God's blessings on his own life. You would think that this would lead to a full life.

Something happened that kept Solomon from living a full life. Something happened that led to him living an empty life. Something happened that caused him to get to the end of his life and say, *"Yea, I hated all my labour which I had taken under the sun…"* Something happened that would cause this man to live under the greatest blessings of God to a point where he would say, *"Vanity of vanities, saith the Preacher, vanity of vanities; all is vanity."*

What was it that brought Solomon to the point where his life was empty? The answer is clearly seen in Ecclesiastes 2. Thirty-four times you see the word *"I."* Fourteen times you see the word *"me."* The thing that made Solomon's life so empty was that his life was all about *"I"* and *"me."* Everything he built, he built for himself. Everything he obtained, he obtained for himself. Everything he conquered, he conquered for himself. Solomon became so focused on himself that he lost the focus of what truly builds a full life. Instead, he made his life empty because it was all about him. When he got old, everything seemed empty as he said, *"…all is vanity."* Yes, all is vanity because he made it about himself, and when you make everything about yourself, you are emptying your life of anything of worth.

Marriage will be empty if you make it all about you. This is a reason many look at marriage as something bad, because their marriage is all about them. You get upset because your spouse is not meeting your needs. You are unhappy because you feel they make everything in the marriage about them. You don't like it when you feel that your spouse must always think they are right. You get upset at your spouse because everything has to be done their way. You will never have a fulfilling marriage until you make your marriage about your spouse. Every marriage that is empty is a marriage where each spouse lives for themselves.

If you want your ministry to be empty, make your ministry about you. When pastor's make their ministry about them and what people think of them, they are building a ministry that will be empty at the end. When church members make their ministry about themselves, they are going to see the ministry as empty and unfulfilling.

You must be careful in every area of your life that you don't fall into the trap of making life about you. When everything is about "me" and "I," you are building an empty life. When you place your life to the side and do everything for God and others, you will find at the end of your life that life is truly fulfilling. Those who live full lives are those who made life about God and others. Learn to take the "I's" and "me's" out of your conversations and life, and you will find life is truly great.

An Apple Tree Among the Trees

Song of Solomon 2:3

"*As the apple tree among the trees of the wood, so is my beloved among the sons. I sat down under his shadow with great delight, and his fruit was sweet to my taste.*"

In the verse above, the wife says that her husband was "*As the apple tree among the trees...*" I like this because out of all the trees in the forest, the one to whom she was married stood out to her. Yes, there were other men around her, but to this lady her husband was the only one she noticed. She was so focused on her husband that she didn't give time to the rest of the "*trees of the wood.*"

Every married person should have the same mentality concerning their spouse that this lady had about her husband. I'm afraid that too many times married people are looking in the forest for someone else instead of focusing on what they have. Many married people don't see the benefits of their own spouse because they are looking at all the other trees in the forest. This little verse has several lessons that every married person needs to apply to their marriage.

First, don't get wrapped up in all the others and not see the benefits of what you do have. The lady in this verse was focused on what her husband gave to her. She wasn't trying to see how much better all the others were for she was solely focused on her own spouse. If you're not careful, you will miss the good of your own spouse because you are too busy comparing them to everyone else. Don't ever compare your spouse to others. If you will look at the good that your spouse provides for you, you won't ever fall for the trap of comparing them to others.

Second, you can't see the weaknesses of the others in the forest. The apple tree is not a pretty tree. I don't know what the other trees were like in this forest that this lady was talking about, but I'm sure she could have easily seen them as better trees than the apple tree. One thing you must always remember is that the other trees at which you are looking will have their own flaws. They may seem pretty at a distance, but when you get closer you will find their flaws just like you found the flaws in your spouse after you got married. Going to someone else is not the answer. The answer is to realize that others have their flaws as well.

Third, the best way to stay focused on your spouse is to see the good they give you. This lady saw the love of her husband and how he provided for her. If you will look at your spouse, you will find that they have much good that they are providing. Stop focusing on the negative. You will never see the good in your spouse if all you do is focus not the negative. Look at the fruit of your spouse. See what being married to your spouse has done for you. If you will take your eyes off yourself, you will see that your spouse has a lot of merits from which you have benefited.

Friend, every person who is married will eventually see the flaws in their spouse. Don't let those discovered flaws keep you from seeing the fruit from their tree. If you will choose to look at the fruit of being married to your spouse, you can get to the point where you look at your spouse as an apple tree among the trees.

Gateways to Protect

Proverbs 4:27

"Turn not to the right hand nor to the left: remove thy foot from evil."

There are four areas in your life that are the gateway to your future. Each of these gateways will determine what becomes of your future. You would think with something so powerful that people would protect those gateways with every part of their being. What I have found is that many times the most unprotected parts of our lives are the parts that influence us the most.

In the last five verses of Proverbs 4, God shows us these gateways that we are to protect. God says in the verse above, *"Turn not to the right hand nor to the left..."* In other words, you must stay straight in these four areas. Let me show you these gateways in your life that you must protect.

First, you must protect the gateway of your heart. Proverbs 4:23 says, *"Keep thy heart with all diligence; for out of it are the issues of life."* Your heart is the hidden part that nobody can see. It is the inner thoughts that you think. The heart is the desires that you have, and the private meditations that you think about. You must protect what you allow to influence your heart. The people with whom you associate will affect your heart. I often say that other than the person you marry, the friends whom you choose will influence you more than anything else. Many people have been ruined by wrong friends. Your friends influence your heart, and whoever influences your heart will determine what you do. You must protect who you allow to be your friends for that is the gateway to your heart.

Second, you must protect the gateway of your mouth. Proverbs 4:24 says, *"Put away from thee a froward mouth, and perverse lips put far from thee."* What you say will determine what people think about you. Far too often we become flippant about the words we say when we should be extremely cautious about our words. Guard the gateway of your mouth and don't say things that you would regret later in life. Don't say things that you wouldn't want everyone to hear.

Third, you must protect the gateway of your eyes. Proverbs 4:25 says, *"Let thine eyes look right on, and let thine eyelids look straight before thee."* What you see goes straight into your mind. Your mind is like a hard drive that stores everything you see. Be very careful about making sure you read and watch the right things. All it takes is one book that teaches something wrong to influence your mind for wrong. All it takes is one look at a wrong picture for your mind to begin imagining thoughts you should never think.

Fourth, you must protect the gateway of your feet. Proverbs 4:26 says, *"Ponder the path of thy feet, and let all thy ways be established."* Let me caution you to only go to the places where you would want Christ to see you. Every place you go you are telling people that you identify with it. The places you go will eventually influence you for right or wrong.

Friend, these four gateways must be protected with all of your being. Don't be flippant with them, but guard them as they are the gateways that influence your future. If you want a good future, you must only allow right influences in each of these gateways.

First Response

Isaiah 38:2

"Then Hezekiah turned his face toward the wall, and prayed unto the LORD,"

The verse above is Hezekiah's first response when he was told that he was going to die. After all that Hezekiah did in bringing Israel back to God, I'm sure he was a little confused and maybe angry that God would take his life. Instead of getting mad at God or doing something he would later regret, he went to God and poured his heart out to Him with his desire to have more life given to him. God heard the prayer of Hezekiah and gave him fifteen more years.

Oftentimes our first response to adverse circumstances is not the best. Once the shock of the initial wave of adverse circumstance is over, what we do just may determine what God will do. There are some in the Scriptures whose first response was the opposite of Hezekiah's, and the result was also the opposite. There are several times in your life when you need to make sure that you have the proper first response.

When sickness comes, your first response should be to pray. Hezekiah was about to die from a sickness, and instead of running to the doctor or health advisor, he ran to the One Who could change his health. I'm not against a person going to the doctor. In fact, I believe it is wise to visit a doctor when you are sick; however, your first response should be to run to God when you are sick. Since when is it right to run to man before you run to God? Maybe the reason many don't see God do something in their health is because they use Him as a last resort when God wants to be your first response.

When you disagree with God, your first response should be to go to Him. It is interesting that Hezekiah disagreed with God, and in his disagreement he didn't quit serving the LORD or run to his friends to complain; instead, he went to God to give his complaint. You are going to have times in your life when you disagree with God. That is simply human nature; however, when you disagree with Him you need to tell Him about it. Quitting the Christian life is not going to help you or make things better. Complaining to your pastor or friends is not going to change one thing. The only way you are going to change your disagreement with God is to go talk to Him. Isn't it interesting that we tell people to go directly to the person with whom they disagree, but we completely avoid talking to God when we disagree with Him? When God does something that you disagree with, go to Him and talk to Him about it. It just might be that you can change God's mind as Hezekiah did.

When tragedy hits, your first response should be to go to God. What happened to Hezekiah was a tragedy. No, he didn't die, but he was about ready to die. When tragedy comes your way, go to God. He is the One Who can help you through your tragedy. Your pastor certainly can help, but he cannot help like God can. In times of tragedy make running to God your first response.

Christian, you are going to have to totally retrain yourself when these moments come. It is natural to go to man or respond adversely in these times, but you must make going to God your first response. He is the only One Who can help you in these times, so don't waste the time you have doing things that can't change your circumstances. The quicker you get to God, the quicker you can see a resolution to your problem.

Holding God's Hand

Isaiah 42:6

"I the LORD have called thee in righteousness, and will hold thine hand, and will keep thee, and give thee for a covenant of the people, for a light of the Gentiles;"

What an endearing statement this verse makes when it says, *"I the LORD...will hold thine hand."* This should show the closeness that God has for every Christian. When I think of holding someone's hand, I think of holding the hand of my wife and daughter. I do this because I am close to them and love them. When I think of God holding our hand there are a couple of thoughts that come to mind.

First, God holds our hand because He loves us. Just like a husband and wife or a parent and child hold hands because they love each other; likewise, God holds our hand because He loves us. Christian, it doesn't matter what you have done, God still loves you. When my daughter has done wrong and I've had to correct her, I did not stop holding her hand. No, in fact I would hold her hand to assure her of my love. Knowing that God loves us enough to hold our hand should comfort and encourage you no matter what you have done in life.

Second, holding one's hand shows that you are not afraid to be associated with them. Oftentimes my wife and I hold hands in public, and one of the reasons we hold hands is because we want to show everyone that we are together. You wouldn't hold the hand of a complete stranger. Likewise, you wouldn't hold the hand of someone with whom you would not want to identify. You hold the hand of someone to show you are not ashamed for it to be known that you are with them. Get this, God is not afraid to show that He is with you. When nobody else wants to be with you, God holds your hand to show everyone that He is with you. When everyone else is ashamed of you and wants nothing to do with you, God will hold your hand to show you that He loves you and identifies with you.

Third, God holds our hand to assure us we are safe in times of insecurity. When my daughter is a bit scared, she will immediately reach for my hand to be assured everything is fine. By holding my hand she can feel that I am not shaking or scared. She feels the steadiness of my hand, and that gives her assurance during a time of insecurity. I love this because when you are scared, God will hold your hand. When you're scared of the visit to the doctor, God will hold your hand. When you're scared to hear what the lawyer will say to you, God will hold your hand. When you're scared to face the accusers, God will hold your hand. When you're scared to face the bill collectors, God will hold your hand. When you're scared to walk through the shadow of death, God will hold your hand. No matter what you are afraid of, if you will look beyond the fear you will feel there is a hand in yours, and that hand is the hand of God.

Fourth, God holds our hand to protect us from danger. It is common that a parent will hold the hand of their child when they are walking through danger to keep the child from hurting themselves. That is what God says He does for us. He holds our hand to "keep" us in times of danger. No matter what danger you face, God will hold your hand to guide you in the threat of danger.

Fifth, God holds our hand to guide us through life. God wants to guide us to the promises He has for us. Friend, if you will just yield to the guiding hand of God, you will find that He will lead you to places of blessings.

Aren't you glad that God holds your hand? Right now take some time and thank God that He is willing to hold your hand. Let me also encourage you never to run from the hand of God. The same hand that is there to do all the things mentioned above is also there to punish you if you run from Him. Let God's hand be endearing in your relationship with Him.

A Pleasant Bruise

Isaiah 53:10

"Yet it pleased the LORD to bruise him; he hath put him to grief: when thou shalt make his soul an offering for sin, he shall see his seed, he shall prolong his days, and the pleasure of the LORD shall prosper in his hand."

"Now, that's going to leave a bruise." This is what we say after we have hit a part of our body on something hard. The next day you find a big ugly bruise on the spot that you hit. The thing about a bruise is that it is only temporary. The bruise will heal and leave no damage.

The verse above says, *"Yet it pleased the LORD to bruise him..."* This verse is saying that God the Father was pleased to bruise His Son, Jesus Christ. The bruising that Jesus took was temporary for Him, but it was eternal for us. It pleased the Father to bruise His Son because He knew that the bruising would provide a way for the restoration of fellowship with mankind. God the Father knew that when He bruised His Son, that bruising would allow you and I to be able to have a relationship with Him.

Moreover, the Son allowed the Father to bruise Him. It is amazing to me that Jesus allowed the Father to hurt Him so that we could have fellowship with the Father. Not only would the bruising allow fellowship with the Father once again, but it would also allow us to have a relationship with Jesus Christ. When the Father told the Son that He would have to bruise Him so the world could have a relationship restored to them, the Son told the Father to go ahead.

How was this bruising administered? It says in the verse above, *"when thou shalt make his soul an offering for sin."* Christian, this was not just a normal bruise, for this bruise would be administered through death. Jesus had to die so that we could have a relationship with Him and the Father. This is nothing short of astounding! The Father would have to bruise His Son Jesus Christ by killing Him and making Him the payment for our sins. Jesus Christ had to yield to the Father's administering of this payment. Why would they go through all of this? They went through this because They loved the world. Yes, Jesus Christ became the offering for sin so that you could go to Heaven. He was willing to do all of this simply because He loved you.

Here is the good thing. The bruise is not lethal. Yes, Jesus died, but it was a bruise. That bruise only lasted for three days and three nights. On Sunday morning when Jesus rose from the dead, the bruise was gone. The sins of mankind were paid forever. That is why it pleased the LORD to bruise Jesus.

Futhermore, it pleased the LORD to bruise Jesus because that bruise also bruised the head of Satan. Genesis 3:15 says, "...*it shall bruise thy head, and thou shalt bruise his heel.*" A bruised head is lethal. The bruising Jesus took was to pay for our eternity, but it was also so that we could have victory over Satan. Satan's power died when Jesus overcame the bruising.

Christian, I point all this out because we need to be regularly reminded of what Jesus did for us. Because Jesus was bruised, you have victory through Him. Let me encourage you to think about this throughout the day, and take some time to thank God that He was willing to be bruised for you.

I Will Glory

Jeremiah 9:24

"*But let him that glorieth glory in this, that he understandeth and knoweth me, that I am the LORD which exercise lovingkindness, judgment, and righteousness, in the earth: for in these things I delight, saith the LORD.*"

God is very clear in the Scriptures that man is not to glory in man. Jeremiah 9:23 says, "*Thus saith the LORD, Let not the wise man glory in his wisdom, neither let the mighty man glory in his might, let not the rich man glory in his riches:*" God knew very well that men like to glory in what they know, what they can do and how much money they have. Very simply, man is not to point to himself at all.

As God always does, He gives us something in which we can glory. The verse above says that if you are going to glory in something, God should be the subject of your glory. Position is not something in which you should glory. The magnificence of one's ministry should not be the focus of your glory. A man's titles should not be the focus of your glory. Only God deserves all glory. In the verse above, God makes it very clear in what we should glory.

First, glory in the fact that you understand and know God. Understanding and knowing God will only come through spending time with Him. You will never know God if you don't spend time in His Word. You will never know God if you don't spend time talking to Him in prayer. You will never know God and understand Him unless you spend time serving with Him in the ministry. If you are not doing any of these things, you have nothing in which to glory.

Second, glory in the lovingkindness of God. This is interesting because the only way you will understand God's lovingkindness is if you have sinned, and He had to be loving and kind to bring you back to Him. In other words, knowing about God's lovingkindness so that you can glory in it only means that you are a sinner who truly has nothing in which you can glory. Your worthlessness was made worthy through God's lovingkindness. You are not anything of yourself, but you are only something because of God, and that is worthy of glory.

Third, glory in the fact that God exercises judgment. You will only understand this by going through trials. When you have served God and seen the world come after you, only after a time of suffering will you see God judge those who have tried to hurt your efforts to serve Him. Again, you are glorying in God because you had no part in bringing justice to the wicked.

Fourth, glory in God's righteousness. This is nothing short of the cross of Calvary. You are not righteous on your own, but you have only had righteousness imputed to your record through the shed blood of Jesus Christ. If we try to glory in our righteousness, there is nothing worthy of glory. Our righteousness is as filthy rags, but it was the righteousness of Jesus that allowed Him to die for us so we can have his righteousness applied to our record when we receive Him as Saviour.

Friend, when you look at these areas where we can glory, you will see that we truly have nothing of our own in which we can glory. Everything you have is because of God. Make your life one that points to God. If you ever try to glory in yourself, God will take you down for He will share His glory with no man. Take the time today to think about these areas, and glory in these areas by telling others about how good God has been to you.

The Iron Furnace

Jeremiah 11:3-4

"And say thou unto them, Thus saith the LORD God of Israel; Cursed be the man that obeyeth not the words of this covenant, Which I commanded your fathers in the day that I brought them forth out of the land of Egypt, from the iron furnace, saying, Obey my voice, and do them, according to all which I command you: so shall ye be my people, and I will be your God:"

When God brought the children of Israel out of Egypt, He brought them out to return no more. One would never expect Israel to have a desire to go back to the land of Egypt, but their desire to go back seemed to plague them for several years.

In the verse above, God reminds Israel that Egypt was an *"iron furnace."* These are strong words. Iron was symbolic of severe slavery or captivity. This wording was to remind them of the shackles that they were under in the land of Egypt. God went further to remind them what Egypt was to them by using the word *"furnace."* The furnace was used to destroy and kill. You'll remember the fiery furnace into which the three Hebrew children were thrown. The furnace was a place to completely destroy after death. It is equivalent to a furnace that a body is put in for cremation; it turns the body into powder. God was saying that Egypt was a place that enslaved them to destroy them. He reminded them that going back to Egypt was going back to the slavery that would cremate them.

A Christian must be careful about desiring to go back to the world. I fear many forget what the world was like before they got saved. Many Christians forget the slavery into which the world put them. They forget the shackles of sin that bound them. They forget how sin was a furnace that literally cremated their dreams and life. The brokenness in which sin left them is often forgotten. How tragic that many Christians forget the iron furnace from which they came; the bondage into which the world put them.

Years ago when I was a teenager, I worked at a paper factory with men who often tried to get me to party with them. They would talk about going out on the weekend and getting drunk, or "smashed" as they put it. I would go back to work on Monday morning and hear them talk of their weekend escapades as if it was something I missed. Then I reminded them that my weekend was not filled with hugging a toilet on Sunday from the recovery of a drunken stupor. I reminded them that I didn't have to deal with a hangover or have to wonder what I did during my weekend because I was sober the whole time. Though they tried to play up their lifestyle, I simply reminded them that their lifestyle brought bondage.

Friend, don't ever forget the iron furnace of the world. Don't ever think that you are missing out on something the world has to offer. The world is an iron furnace that not only wants to enslave you, but enslave you to the point that it will cremate every dream you have. It will cremate your future and your family. Many people have come out of sin with broken lives and broken families. Oh, please take this warning seriously. The world is an iron furnace. Everything the world offers comes with shackles. Those shackles will bind you until everything you have is cremated by the world's furnace.

I challenge you to obey God's Word. God's Word keeps you from the iron furnace. God's Word will bring you joy and happiness. God's Word will help your dreams come to reality. If the world has its shackles of sin on you now, I encourage you to get help to overcome those sins. If you're considering the world's offers, I beg you to look at everyone who has taken that offer and you will find that they live a life shackled by that sin. The only life that will give you complete freedom is the life of serving God.

Friendly Fire

Jeremiah 26:8

"Now it came to pass, when Jeremiah had made an end of speaking all that the LORD had commanded him to speak unto all the people, that the priests and the prophets and all the people took him, saying, Thou shalt surely die."

One would wonder why Jeremiah would keep going. When you read the Book of Jeremiah, you see that Jeremiah was constantly maligned and attacked. He was not attacked or maligned by the enemy; it was friendly fire. He was attacked by his own countrymen. It was his fellow prophets who tried to discredit what he said. When he was thrown in a pit to die, it was not foreign enemies who put him into the pit to die, but it was his own people whom he was trying to help that put him into the pit to die. Very few people would be able to take the abuse that Jeremiah faced and stay on message and not compromise.

I was recently having lunch with a person who expressed to me that they were tired of all the "infighting" in Christianity. They felt that the infighting was needless. It was interesting as I talked to this individual that they felt those standing for truth were the problem. They felt that their "divisive stand" was causing division among Christians. Yet, when I continued to talk to them about standing for truth and not compromising, they wholeheartedly agreed that compromise is everywhere. This amazed me because they were blaming those standing for truth as the divisive one's and not the compromisers who accuse those standing for truth of being the troublemakers.

Friendly fire is always the worst way at which to be shot. It is not that you enjoy being shot at from anyone, but you sure don't expect to have to defend yourself from your own. You would expect that your own would stand with you as you stand for truth. Yet, I find that the majority of the time it is friendly fire that discredits and maligns those who stand for truth. Just like

Jeremiah, you must not allow friendly fire to get you off message. You must always stand for truth even when your own are attacking you.

If you are the one being maligned and attacked by friendly fire, let me encourage you not to compromise. Someone must stand for truth! Standing for truth is never easy, but if truth is going to prevail then you must keep trumpeting it. Don't let the misguided attacks cause you to quit or compromise. There are generations who follow you who need you to continue to stand so they can know what is truth. It may hurt when those whom you call your friends shoot at you for your stand, but you must confide in God and let His presence be your comfort.

To those who are tired of all the "infighting," let me encourage you not to attack and discredit those who stand for truth. They are not the one's who have changed. They are not the problem. You need to discredit those who are compromising. You will always find that compromisers have a way of painting those who tell the truth as the problem because they won't negotiate or change. Let me ask you, how do you negotiate truth? You can't! Truth is never up for negotiation. What you need to get tired of is those who want to water down Christianity. You need to get tired of those who malign people who firmly stand for truth. The truth bearers are not the problem, it's the compromisers who are the problem.

Don't be a part of the friendly fire. When someone stands for truth, support them. It's never comfortable to stand for truth, and that is why you must stand with those who stand. When friendly fire comes your way, don't change! Always stay on message and don't let the friendly fire sidetrack you from trumpeting truth.

Where Are Your Prophets?

Jeremiah 37:19

"Where are now your prophets which prophesied unto you, saying, The king of Babylon shall not come against you, nor against this land?"

Jeremiah asked King Zedekiah a question that needed to be answered. He asked, *"Where are now your prophets which prophesied unto you..."* These prophets prophesied against Jeremiah. These prophets said that Babylon would not come and take Jerusalem. These prophets said that Jeremiah's preaching was too extreme. Yet, when Jeremiah asked Zedekiah where his prophets were, Babylon was outside the gates of Jerusalem.

Zedekiah, where are your prophets when your country is overtaken by the Chaldeans? Zedekiah, where are your prophets when your sons are killed right before your eyes? Zedekiah, where are your prophets when your eyes are plucked out of their sockets? Zedekiah, where are your prophets when your house is burnt with fire? Zedekiah, where are your prophets as you sit bound with chains in a Babylonian prison? Zedekiah, where are your prophets when the walls of Jerusalem are broken down?

I bet you wish you had listened to Jeremiah when he told you to cleanse your ways. I bet you wish you had fired the false prophets who prophesied peace when war was at your doorstep. I bet you wish you had done what was right the first time, but now it's too late. Now you sit in a prison cell mourning the loss of your family. Now you sit in a prison cell with your eyes plucked from your sockets never again to see another sunrise or beautiful flower. Now you realize that Jeremiah wasn't so divisive or hard, because now you realize what he said was true. But now it's a little too late.

Sadly, this story is played out in the lives of Christians over and over again. I watch Christians who think they know better than the man of God who warns them that what they are doing will lead to hurt and destruction. I watch Christians listen to the compromising preachers who call out those preachers who preach the truth and say they are angry preachers who have an agenda.

Yes, we do have an agenda. Our agenda is to save your family from heartache. Our agenda is to keep your daughter from the hands of a promiscuous young man. Our agenda is to make sure you happily grow old. Our agenda is to make sure your children walk down the aisle of marriage as a virgin, pure and innocent. Our agenda is to keep your mind from being controlled by lust. Our agenda is to make sure you never see the backdoor of sin. Our agenda is to make sure that you are not the next illustration of sin's effect. Our agenda is to preach in such a manner that you won't have to look back at your life with regret.

Friend, where are these preachers who told you to lower your standards when you walk into the preachers office with a daughter who is pregnant as a teenager? Where are these preachers who told you that casual living is the way we do things today, as you sit in a divorce court because your spouse was too casual with their work partner or a friend at church? Where are these compromising preachers who preached grace without truth when sin has touched your life and left its devastation?

Christian, you would be wise to listen to the Jeremiah's whom God has placed in your life. The preachers who tell the truth may not always be as smooth as the compromising preacher, but they are telling the truth, and they are trying to keep you from facing the heartache that Zedekiah saw. Don't disdain the Jeremiah's in your life. Listen to them, for they only want the best for your life.

Given to Appetite

Proverbs 23:2

"And put a knife to thy throat, if thou be a man given to appetite."

Controlling one's appetite is one of the hardest things to do. Whether the appetite is for food, money or things, once an appetite is established it is hard to control it. It is better to never create the appetite than to start it and try to control it.

The verse above is talking about controlling your appetite. God says that if you are sitting down at a king's table, put a knife to your throat and don't become enamored with the delicacies on the table. God is teaching that once you create the appetite it will be hard to control it. So, it is much better to never put yourself in the place where it can be created than to have to try and curb your appetite. Let me give you some suggestions on this subject.

First, don't put yourself in a place where you can't afford the appetite. One of the things I despise is going window shopping. Window shopping is one of the most wasteful things a person can do. When you window shop, you are looking at things you cannot buy because you can't afford them. I've always said that you should never go look at something that you cannot afford. If you can't afford a house in a certain neighborhood, you would be wise not to drive through that neighborhood if you are given to appetite. If you can't afford clothing at a certain store, don't go to that store. This could be said about a car or any other possession.

If you are a person given to appetite, you will figure out a way to satisfy your appetite. Many people have put themselves into such debt that they can't afford because they purchased something from an appetite greater than they could afford. Just because you figure out a way to satisfy your appetite doesn't mean you can afford it. Stay away from places where the appetite created is more than you can afford.

Second, don't assume you can control your appetite. Most of us feel that we can control our appetites, but we truly have a hard time doing so. Don't underestimate the power of your appetite. You may initially think you can control it, but the mind has a way of working on you to get you to the point where you try to satisfy an appetite. Always consider what you can't afford before going into any place, for every place will create some appetite.

Third, if your appetite is out of control, get some help. An appetite out of control is an addiction. It is hard to admit that we are addicted to something. We often equate addiction with alcohol or drugs, but there are people who are addicted to far more things than these. If you have told yourself more than twice that you are going to stop something but you're still doing it, you are addicted and need some help. Your appetite is out of control, and only help from a spiritual source will curtail that appetite.

Friend, take God's warning about controlling your appetite in every area. Don't place yourself in any area or situation where you can create an appetite you can't afford. Better yet, don't ever place yourself in a situation that will create an appetite that will hinder you. Every person is given to appetite, so avoid those appetites that you can't afford or don't need.

Sin's Last Word

Lamentation 1:1
"How doth the city sit solitary, that was full of people! how is she become as a widow! she that was great among the nations, and princess among the provinces, how is she become tributary!"

Sin's last word is much different than it promised. Sin is one of the biggest liars you will ever hear. It promises dreams, but gives you heartache. It promises everything, but gives you nothing. It promises the world, but gives you bondage. Sin's promise is truly empty.

Jeremiah laments what sin had done to the people of God. The Book of Lamentations is truly the last word of sin. Jeremiah shows that the promises of sin never came through. Certainly, they enjoyed their sin for a bit, but when the last word is spoken you see a people who realized the emptiness of sin's promise. Let's look at the last word of sin.

Sin's last word is that it will leave you alone. One of the promises of sin is that it gives you a lot of friends, but when you look at the verse above you realize that sin left these people alone. Sin left a city that used to be filled with people a solitary place. Sin left the city a ghost town. This was not what sin promised, but these people found out that sin leaves you all alone.

Likewise, sin will not give you the friends that you think it will. Yes, they may come in the beginning, but when all is said and done, you will be alone to deal with the affects of your sin. I have watched many people who accepted sin's invitation find that when their sin was revealed, the friends they had were gone. Don't believe sin's promise of friendship, for sin's last word is loneliness.

Sin's last word is that it will leave you in sorrow. Jeremiah makes the statement that the city had *"become as a widow."* In other words, they were grieving their loss. Sin promised them so much but left them with nothing. Sin will do the same thing for you. It will promise you everything but it will leave you grieving your losses. Sin always leaves a person to wonder, "What if…" What a terrible way to live the rest of your life! God wants His children to enjoy their life *"more abundantly."* (John 10:10) Friend, you can live the abundant life if you will stay away from sin, but if you let sin have its way in your life the last word will leave you grieving what you could have had.

The last word of sin is that it leaves you serving. Notice that the city had *"become tributary."* Sin promised them that they would be in control of their own lives, but the last word of sin left them serving sin. When you accept sin's invitation, you are accepting the chains that come with sin. Sin eventually controls you. When you want to quit, it will keep you coming back. The freedom it promised will never be realized. Don't ever think that sin will give you more freedom than doing right. Once you start down the road of sin, you will then have to deal with the heartache of its servitude.

Christian, don't let sin have the last word in your life. The last word of sin is always heartache; whereas, the last word of doing right is an abundant life. Now is the time to deal with your sin. You can stop sin from having the last word in your life by forsaking it now. Don't be the next statistic of sin. Whatever sin you have allowed in your life, take care of it today by confessing it to God and forsaking it!

False Assurances

Ezekiel 11:3

"Which say, It is not near; let us build houses: this city is the caldron, and we be the flesh."

The prophets in Ezekiel's day were lying prophets. They knew very well that Ezekiel's prophecy was correct, but they gave the people a false assurance by telling them Jerusalem would not be taken captive. They said that Jerusalem was a caldron, and they were the flesh. A caldron is a vessel used to boil flesh over a fire. You would put the flesh in the caldron, and hang the vessel on a hook over the fire. Though fire would heat up the caldron, the flesh inside would not be burnt. These prophets were saying that no matter what happened outside the walls of Jerusalem, they were safe inside those walls. Though what these prophets prophesied was comforting to the people, all they did was give them a false assurance which eventually led to their demise.

Many Christians have thought of themselves like that caldron. No, they may not have exactly used that analogy, but in their mind they had the same false assurance that Jerusalem had. I look at this verse and I see three false assurances many people have about their sin.

The first false assurance is that it won't happen to them. Jerusalem thought they were safe inside the caldron of the walls. They thought it would never happen to them. Many Christians have ruined their lives in sin using this mentality. For whatever reason they believe it won't happen to them, and they rest on that false assurance. You may think that sin will not touch you, but you must always realize that sin has a price that must be paid.

The second false assurance is, "I'm not like everyone else." This is nothing short of pride. This comes from the mentality that you think you are smarter than everyone else. This comes from the thought that others were not as smart as you, and that you have contrived a plan to enjoy your sin so that God won't punish you. Friend, you are like everyone else. You are not smarter than those who succumbed before you. If you have sin in your life and this devotional is simply a bunch of words that you're reading, then you have fallen for this false assurance. Sin is not a respecter of persons, and you will have to pay sin's price.

The third false assurance is, "We are stronger than our sin." This is haughtiness to the core. This comes from the mentality that you have everything under control, but what you don't realize is that sin has you under control. You may feel that you're in control, but sin allows you to feel that way until its payment comes due.

There is only one caldron in which you are safe, and that is the caldron of Jesus Christ. When you live according to His Word, you will be safe no matter what goes on around you. Living in Christ is a caldron that the fire cannot touch. Christian, I encourage you to live inside of that caldron. Sin's caldron is weak, and the fire around it will get to you. Yet, the caldron of Christ has been tried and tested over time, and the results show us that the fire cannot hurt you as long as you live inside of that caldron.

I encourage you to look at which caldron you are in, and make sure that Christ is the only One in Whom you trust. Don't live in the false assurances of sin, but let Christ's Word be the confidence in which you put your trust.

Parenting Mistakes

Proverbs 29:15

"The rod and reproof give wisdom: but a child left to himself bringeth his mother to shame."

One of the hardest things a person will do in life is be a parent. Parenting is not easy. If someone knew the formula for turning out good children, that person would be wealthy. The problem with child rearing is that each child has their own personality, and that personality makes them unique in every way.

When it comes to child rearing, there are some principles that help in parenting. The Scriptures are filled with parenting advice that if followed children will turn out for the good. The verse above is one of those verses that gives some parenting advice. God shows us some mistakes that parents make in rearing their children. If you will learn the principles God is teaching in this verse, you will have a greater chance of your children doing right. Let me show you three mistakes from this verse that you should avoid as a parent.

The first mistake is using the rod alone. Notice the verse above says, *"The rod and reproof..."* A parent who only uses punishment without the reproof that comes with punishment is setting their child up to become angry with them. Parents should punish their children, but their children need to know why they are being punished. Every time you punish your child, it should be a teaching moment to teach them about life. Punishment alone will drive your child away from you.

The second mistake is using reproof alone. Reproof without punishment does not teach the child that sin has consequences. Many parents think it is cruel to punish their children, but if they don't learn consequences come with wrong actions, you are setting your children up for much heartache. I believe it is important to reprove your children and teach them why something is wrong, but when they do wrong they also need to learn the consequences that are a result of doing wrong.

The third mistake is spending time with your children, but not reproving and punishing them when they do wrong. The spectrum in this area goes both ways. Some parents reprove and punish but they don't spend time with their children, and then there are other parents who spend time with their children but don't punish and reprove them. All three are important to helping your children turn out right. A parent who does not spend any time with their children is a parent who is allowing others to influence over them. The greatest influence on a child should be their parent, and the only way they are going to have the prominent influence is by spending time with their children.

Are you making these common parenting mistakes? Punishment without reproof and lack of time together will cause a child to become foolish. Reproof without punishment and time together will again cause a child to live a foolish life. Punishment and reproof without a parent spending time with their child will bring shame to their parents. All three are important in children choosing a wise life and bringing honor to their parents. Make sure as a parent that you use all three tools to influence your child for right.

A Lovely Song

Ezekiel 33:32

"And, lo, thou art unto them as a very lovely song of one that hath a pleasant voice, and can play well on an instrument: for they hear thy words, but they do them not."

On my computer I have a playlist that has some of my favorite songs that I love to hear. Many times throughout the week I will play this list of songs I enjoy hearing. It is not just the songs, but the artists as well. One of my favorite singers on this list is Bro. Alvin Martinez. His music is Spirit-filled, and his singing touches my heart. There is no doubt that I would say his singing is lovely.

God told Ezekiel that his preaching had become a lovely song to those who were listening. Ezekiel's problem was not that he didn't have a crowd to whom he could preach. The people enjoyed watching his illustrations. They saw him preach the next day after his wife had passed away from a stroke. His preaching was not abrasive as was the Apostle Paul's, but it was a well-displayed sermon like a person who *"can play well on an instrument."*

The problem with these people was that his preaching had become a lovely song that they loved to hear. They would listen to the preaching, but they would go home and do the exact opposite of what he preached. They loved Ezekiel, but they simply came to hear what he would say because they wanted to see his next illustration or hear the eloquence of his preaching. More important than seeing his illustrations, was listening to the sermon. More important than loving the man of God, they should have heeded to the warning of each sermon. Ezekiel would rather these people obeyed the message of his sermon than like his preaching. Though Ezekiel preached exactly what God wanted him to preach, and though he preached exactly how God wanted him to preach, the people wasted the message because they came simply to hear him preach.

Dr. Jack Hyles was my pastor for many years. In this preacher's opinion, Bro. Hyles was the best preacher I have ever heard, and I'm not alone with this summation. Yet, I'm amazed that though Dr. Hyles was one of the greatest voices that preached against compromise in our day, many who heard him are doing the exact opposite of what he preached. Sadly, I believe what happened is that many people came to hear this man of God preach, but they only came because his preaching was a lovely song to them. They did not come to heed his preaching; they came to be in the presence of one whom God used greatly.

Has preaching become a lovely song to you? Do you listen to your pastor or to your favorite preacher because their preaching is as a lovely song? Is it that you like their humor, stories or their delivery that draws you to listen to their preaching? It would be sad that preaching is nothing more than a lovely song to which you listen. It would be sad that you listen to your pastor every week, a man whom you love and enjoy listening to, but don't heed the content of his sermons.

Be careful that you don't allow preaching to become a lovely song. Don't miss the content of the sermon for the beauty of the delivery. Don't listen to the sermon just because you enjoy preaching and walk away and do the complete opposite of what you just heard. God has not given you the opportunity to hear a truth from your favorite preacher just so you can walk away and do the opposite. Every time you listen to preaching, listen to it so you can correct what you're doing wrong. Make the sermon more than a lovely song. Make it the alarm that causes you to correct the things in your life that are wrong. Don't be guilty of hearing what you are supposed to do, but walk away and do the opposite. Don't just listen to preaching, but respond to its message and correct what it tells you to correct.

When the Glory of God Shines

Ezekiel 43:2

"And, behold, the glory of the God of Israel came from the way of the east: and his voice was like a noise of many waters: and the earth shined with his glory."

Every Christian should desire to let the glory of God shine through their life. Too often we have Christians trying to receive the glory when all glory should be given to God. There is nothing wrong with honoring a man, but man should never receive more glory than God. I find in the verse above that several things happen when a person allows God's glory to shine through their life.

First, God's voice will be clear when you let His glory shine in your life. Notice that Ezekiel recognized God's voice clearly. It was very distinct to Him. He could tell you what it sounded like. When a Christian allows God's glory to shine in their life, they will clearly know what God wants them to do. They won't wonder about God's will for their life, for God's voice will be clearly understood. If a person is having a hard time knowing God's will for their life, they would be wise to see if they are letting God's glory shine clearly in their life. The more you give glory to God, the more you will understand what God wants you to do in your life.

Second, God's presence will be seen in your life when you let His glory shine in your life. Verse 3 shows that God's glory was evident in the house of the LORD. The more you point to Christ, the more you will see God's glory shine on your life. Moses pointed to God, and in return God allowed His glory to shine on Moses. When you don't make yourself the issue, you will find that God will shine through you to a darkened and needy world.

Third, when God's glory shines on your life, you will see your worthlessness. When Ezekiel entered God's presence, he fell upon his face because he saw his own worthlessness. You will always find in the Scriptures that those who are in the presence of God don't see how good they are, but they see how bad they are. If you will allow God's glory to shine in your life, you will begin to see your own worthlessness and His righteousness. This is why I find that those who tend to point to themselves often are those who are not living close to the presence of God. God's presence has a way of humbling the best of Christians.

Fourth, God's Spirit will guide you when you let His glory shine in your life. Verse 5 says, *"So the spirit took me up…"* God's Holy Spirit will never point to man. He will only point to Jesus Christ. If you want God's power on your life, you must let His glory shine through you so that He will allow His Holy Spirit to empower you. The empowering of the Holy Spirit will always cause you to point others to Jesus Christ.

Finally, sin will be put away when you let God's glory shine in your life. Verse 9 says, *"Now let them put away their whoredom…"* The Christian will not want any sin in their life when they let God's glory shine. They don't want sin because they know that sin will quench God's glory. Friend, I encourage you to make sure you continually work on removing sin from your life if you want to see God's glory in your life.

Are you letting God's glory shine in your life? Imagine the change that would happen around you if you let God's glory shine. Imagine the change that would happen in your home, church, workplace and surroundings if God's glory was shining on your life. One of the greatest needs of today is for Christians to let God's glory shine in their life. I encourage you to make daily effort to show God's glory in your life. Take yourself off your pedestal of glory and only let God receive the glory for all that happens in your life. It is then that these five things will become evident in your life.

Daniel's Steps to Prosperity

Daniel 6:28

"So this Daniel prospered in the reign of Darius, and in the reign of Cyrus the Persian."

Prosperity is a relative term. What one calls prosperity may not be prosperity for another; however, when God says someone prospers then that would certainly define prosperity across the board. There is one person whom God said prospered, and that person was Daniel. When you study the life of Daniel, you find some very clear steps he took that caused him to prosper.

First, Daniel had a good attitude. Verse 3 says that Daniel had an *"excellent spirit."* It is hard to find someone who has prospered who didn't have a good spirit. I'm not just talking about a good attitude as you go throughout the day, but a good attitude towards life and its goals. You will never prosper if your attitude is negative towards everything. If you have an attitude that says it can't be done, you will never prosper. A good attitude towards the possibility of things happening is imperative if you are going to prosper in life.

Second, Daniel was dependable. It was said about Daniel that *"he was faithful."* He was faithful to his job, and you also find that faithfulness was found in other areas of his life. If you can't be depended upon, don't expect God to help you to prosper. One element you will find in everyone who is prosperous is that they are dependable. They show up for work every day no matter how they feel or what they are facing. Dependability is a must for prosperity.

Third, Daniel had character. When his enemies tried to find fault in him, it was said that *"neither was there any error or fault found in him."* Character is a big ingredient to success. You will find that those who are prosperous throughout life are people who have character. In other words, they do right all the time whether or not anyone is watching. You will never prosper if the only time you do right is when someone is watching.

Fourth, Daniel had a love for God. Daniel's enemies knew that the only way they could destroy him was through his walk with God. Everyday he spent time walking with God. As a Christian, you will only find that God will help you prosper if you spend time with Him each day. Your love for God must be greater than your love for the world. Daniel's love for God caused him to walk with Him on a daily basis.

Fifth, Daniel lived by schedule. After the law was made that they could only pray to the king, Daniel went to the place where he prayed and spent time thanking God and praying *"as he did aforetime."* He didn't do this because of the law, he did this because it was in his schedule. If you live your life off the cuff and let life dictate what you are going to do, prosperity will be hard to find. You will never find success in life until you learn to live by schedule.

Sixth, Daniel had the backbone to stand. When the law was made that he could not talk to God, he was not afraid of facing the lions for his beliefs. Friend, you must have some core beliefs that you are willing to stand for no matter the cost if you are going to be prosperous. A spineless person who only does what the crowd wants will not find success. Those who stand when others will not stand are those who tend to find success.

You will never find prosperity in your life if these six things are not a part of your life. Prosperity may not mean riches, but prosperity does mean success. If you want everything you do to prosper, take these six things and implement them in your daily life.

Before the Departure

Hosea 1:2

"The beginning of the word of the LORD by Hosea. And the LORD said to Hosea, Go, take unto thee a wife of whoredoms and children of whoredoms: for the land hath committed great whoredom, departing from the LORD."

One of the more interesting things that God commanded a prophet to do was to go take a wife of whoredoms. Hosea was an amazing man in that he didn't question God, but he immediately obeyed. God wanted Hosea to take a wife of whoredoms because He knew she would eventually leave Hosea for her lifestyle. Though Hosea would initially save her from this life, she would eventually leave him to go back to her old lifestyle.

God equated His relationship with Israel as a husband and wife. Just like Hosea's wife would depart from him, God said that Israel would depart *"from the LORD."* Using the word *"departing"* is a very strong word because this implies that it was not a mistake, but it was a purposeful choice. It was Israel's choice to leave the LORD.

A Christian never "falls" into sin; they depart into sin. Sin is never an accident; sin is a choice. Too often we want to imply that our sins are a mistake with which we had nothing to do, but that simply is not true. Every time a Christian goes into sin, they chose to go into sin. You can choose to say that you fell into sin, but God's Word says that we depart into sin. Sin is a choice.

David didn't fall into adultery, he chose to commit adultery. Peter didn't fall into denying the LORD, rather he chose to deny the LORD. Ananias and Sapphira didn't fall into lying to the Holy Ghost; they chose to lie to the Holy Ghost. Any time anyone sins, including you, they chose to go into sin. Better yet, they depart into sin. It is a willful act on the part of the Christian to go into sin.

However, before Israel chose to depart into sin, they departed from God in their heart and mind. They thought another lifestyle would be better. They thought other gods could do them better. They thought other commands were better. Before they physically departed to other gods, they had departed in their hearts and mind.

Before a Christian ever departs into sin, they mentally depart from God. Before a Christian's backslidden ways are seen by others, they have already backslidden in their heart. To depart from God means they planned the departure before they actually departed. To depart from God means they lived the other life in their mind before they actually departed to live that life. To depart from God means they saw another lifestyle in their mind that was better than the Christian lifestyle. It all happens in the mind. Before a person ever departs into sin, they have already departed in their mind.

Friend, you must protect your mind. Your mind will come up with imaginations about sin that just are not true. That is why God says in 2 Corinthians 10:5, *"Casting down imaginations, and every high thing that exalteth itself against the knowledge of God, and bringing into captivity every thought to the obedience of Christ;"* You must control what you think so that you don't depart from God in your mind.

Let me simply remind you that no matter what you imagine is better than serving God, it is not! Every other lifestyle will bring heartache and dissatisfaction. Don't allow yourself to depart from God in your heart and mind. Before you ever depart from the LORD and choose to commit some sin, always remember that sin cannot satisfy. It is your choice to stay with God, and the choice to stay with God's lifestyle will bring joy and satisfaction. Don't depart in your heart and mind, for that will eventually bring an actual physical departure from God.

The Silent Killer

Joel 1:12

"The vine is dried up, and the fig tree languisheth; the pomegranate tree, the palm tree also, and the apple tree, even all the trees of the field, are withered: because joy is withered away from the sons of men."

I was recently listening to the late legendary coach Jimmy Valvano give his famous speech in 1993. Jimmy Valvano was the head coach of North Carolina State University who, against all odds, won the 1983 NCAA Basketball Tournament. His team was considered the "Cinderella team." Jimmy V, as he was known, was sick with cancer when he gave this famous speech. He said there were three things people should do every day, and one of those three things was to laugh. These were inspiring words to hear from someone who was fighting cancer.

The verse above says that the vine, fig tree, pomegranate tree and palm tree were drying up and dying because there was no joy *"from the sons of men."* God is teaching that the lack of joy causes things to die. In other words, not having joy is a silent killer. We certainly are concerned about things that kill people, and there are some things over which we have no control, but we do have control over whether or not we are joyful. Being joyful is a choice. You can choose from whence your joy comes.

If I were to tell you that I had a cure for cancer, you would certainly be interested in that cure and especially if you had a family member fighting cancer. If I told you that I know where you can get a cure for multiple sclerosis, you would want to know where to go if you or a loved one were dealing with this horrible disease. Yet, the Scriptures give us a cure from life withering away, and that cure is joy. Life doesn't have to be a drudgery that we must go through. Life can be joyful, and that joy will keep your life from withering away.

Too many churches are places where there is no joy. If you were to walk into the average church, you would find a place that looks and feels more like a funeral service than a church service. Far too often we equate worship with solemnness and no laughter. Yes, there are times when we should be solemn in church, but I believe that church should be a place where God's people smile, laugh and enjoy what He is doing in their midst.

Moreover, your home should be a place where there is joy. If you want the life of your home to continue, you better learn to make it a place of joy. Sadly, more homes are places of fighting and squabbling than they are places of joy. You might find that your children would enjoy being home if they felt that home was a place of joy.

One of the ways you are going to keep joy in your church and home is to keep the drama of life away from them. Certainly, we all have our drama with which we must deal, but it doesn't have to control our atmospheres. Deal with the drama of life, but don't let the drama of life dictate the atmosphere of your home and church.

Furthermore, you can keep the joy in your home and church by laughing. Yes, you can laugh. Laughter is a good medicine. God says in Proverbs 17:22, "*A merry heart doeth good like a medicine...*" Mr. Valvano was right when he said that we should laugh everyday. Laughter is the medicine of life that keeps joy alive.

Friend, let me encourage you keep the silent killer of no joy away from your home and church. Decide to be the one who cheers up every place you go. If you must change your personality, do it for the sake of life. Let joy become a part of your personality, and you will find that the drama of life will not kill the atmosphere of the places you love.

And God Saw Their Works

Jonah 3:10

"And God saw their works, that they turned from their evil way; and God repented of the evil, that he had said that he would do unto them; and he did it not."

There is always hope with God. It does not matter to what depths of sin you have sunk or the shame that your sin has caused, God is always willing to forgive and rebuild a life. God's mercy can reach to any depth and pull anyone out of sin.

Nineveh found this out first hand. God had pronounced judgment against this city because of their wickedness. God sent Jonah to preach against the city and give them one last chance to get right with Him. As we can see from the verse above, they listened to the preaching of the prophet and repented of their sin. The verse says, *"And God saw their works, that they turned from their evil way; and God repented of the evil…"* Nineveh's actions caused God to exercise mercy upon this city. Just as Nineveh saw God's mercy, any person who has sinned can see God's mercy. Let me give you several thoughts that we can glean from this verse.

First, God always gives a last chance to repent before He sends His judgment. God had already determined His judgment, but wanted to give them one more chance to get right. I have found that God always gives a last chance before sending His judgment. What you must be careful of is that you don't always know when it is God's last chance. This is why we must get right the first time God gives us a chance. God is not obligated to give a chance, and He is not obligated to give us more than one chance to get right, so when He gives a chance you should take advantage of it.

Second, words of repentance are not good enough. Notice the verse says, *"And God saw their works…"* It didn't say that God heard their words of repentance, but He *"saw their works."* You can go to God a thousand times and ask God to forgive you, but God's mercy is exercised because of actions and not because of words. Many Christians live on a false assurance of confession when God wants actions to follow up confession. Notice that Proverbs 28:13 says, *"He that covereth his sins shall not prosper: but whoso confesseth and forsaketh them shall have mercy."* God's mercy does not go into action until you take action about your sin.

Third, your actions will always speak louder than your words. God desires action more than He requires words. Yes, God wants to hear you admit that you are sorry for your sin, but His greatest desire is that you back up your words with actions. God is looking to see if you meant what you said. Friend, you cannot fool God. You can tell God that you are sorry, but He looks to see if you change your ways. We can easily fall into the trap of thinking we can pull the wool over God's eyes like we do with mankind, but God knows your heart and sees your action. Don't make the mistake of thinking you can fool God like you have everyone else.

Let me ask you, what are your works saying to God? Do your works compel God to be merciful to you? Every Christian needs God's mercy on a daily basis. Daily live your life showing God through your works that you are serious about doing right. Always remember that it is not always the best Christians who receive God's mercy, but it is those who back up their words of confession with works. Let God see your works of righteousness, and you will experience the mercy of God.

Are Thou Not From Everlasting

Habakkuk 1:12

"Art thou not from everlasting, O LORD my God, mine Holy One? we shall not die. O LORD, thou hast ordained them for judgment; and, O mighty God, thou hast established them for correction."

As Habakkuk testified of the coming judgment of God upon Israel, he paused for a moment to tell of the greatness of God. He posed a question as a statement about the beginnings of God when he says, *"Art thou not from everlasting..."* Yes, he was reminding the children of Israel that the LORD God is not just a god who has come around lately, but He is a God Who has always been in existence. He was testifying of the Deity of God.

As a Christian, you can rejoice in the fact that God is an everlasting God. The comfort and confidence this should bring to you should be tremendous. It should have such an impact on your life that you should never again question God or the lifestyle that He commands you to live. Let me give you some thoughts about God being an everlasting God.

First, nothing is new to God. Whatever problem you face on a daily basis, God knows how to handle that problem. Whatever trial you are going through at this present moment is not something that God has not seen before. Whatever heartache you may be experiencing is not something that God has not helped others with in the past. To say that God is from everlasting is more than the mind can truly comprehend. It should comfort the believer to know that no matter what they face, they have a God Who can help them through it. You don't have to face your problems alone. Instead of going to those who have a beginning with your problems, you should go to the One Who is from everlasting, for He has seen this problem before and knows how to help you no matter how unique your problem may be.

Second, God is not going to run out on you. Because God is from everlasting, that means He is not a storefront shop that sells you something today and is gone tomorrow when you need help with the product. Friend, if God commands you to do something, you can be assured that He will be there when you need Him. God is not a fly-by-night god who commands you to step out by faith and won't be around when you step out. No, when you step out by faith, you will find that God will be there for you to help you through whatever faith has brought your way.

Third, because God is from everlasting, that means He is in control. When you look at the world system, you can sometimes think that everything is falling apart. I'm glad that I serve a God Who is in control. God's plan is working out, and you simply need to rest in the confidence that you are a part of God's plan. Everything that is happening in this world is bringing us to the point when God is going to come back and rapture the saved to Heaven. You need not fret about the world system, God is from everlasting and it is all part of His plan to prepare the world for His coming.

Christian, stop for a bit and think about what an everlasting God truly means to your life. You will find that as you meditate on this thought it will bring a comfort and confidence to help you face every situation in your life. There is no need to be stressed out in life when your God is from everlasting. He is in control, and you don't need to worry or fret for He will help you through your problems if you will simply yield to His guiding hand.

Small Things

Zechariah 4:10

"For who hath despised the day of small things? for they shall rejoice, and shall see the plummet in the hand of Zerubbabel with those seven; they are the eyes of the LORD, which run to and fro through the whole earth."

The power of small things can never be underestimated. Everything big starts out small. It may seem that something so small can be harmless, but some of the deadliest things on Earth are small.

God said in the verse above, *"For who hath despised the day of small things?"* Throughout the Scriptures God used small things to teach big lessons. It was small Zaccheus who Jesus pointed out in a tree so that he could get saved. It was a small piece of fruit that Adam and Eve ate that led to the first sin. God is reminding us in the verse above not to ignore the small things in life. There are several small things I would like to point out that can have a big impact if you ignore them.

First, don't ignore the small sin. Every sin starts out small, but that small sin always grows like a cancer. The small sin you ignore will be the big sin that you deal with later. You may think you can handle the small sin, but that small sin continues to get stronger each day that you don't deal with it.

Second, don't ignore the small time wasters. We often say that we don't have enough time to do things, but this is not true. I have found we always have time to do something, it is simply that we have wasted our time in small increments. One minute here and there can add up to hours. Just a couple of minutes that you waste doing frivolous things can add up to several minutes that you could have used to accomplish something great. Time wasters always come in packages of small minutes. If you will do away with the small packages of time wasters, you will find you will have the time to accomplish everything you need to get done.

Third, don't ignore the small tasks. It is the small tasks that often mess up a big job. Have you ever left off one screw when assembling something thinking that it was unimportant only to find that one screw helped everything to work right? Always remember that the small tasks added up will make big tasks. If all you do is give your attention to the "big" things of life, the small things will be what destroys your potential.

Fourth, don't ignore the small moments of life with people. We often don't absorb every small moment in time we have with someone only to regret it later in life. Friend, every moment with a loved one or friend is important. Don't let distractions keep you from having quality time with people. One day that loved one or friend will be gone and you will wish you gave every small moment the greatest attention you had.

Fifth, don't ignore the "small" people. I am not talking about stature here, I am talking about people whom we consider unimportant. You should be thankful that God didn't consider you a "small" person. Every person is important! Don't allow yourself to come across as someone who is too big to talk to someone. Everyone deserves the same attention. Let the "small" people of your life feel important for you never know how they can help you in the future.

Small things always become big. Every small thing you despise will cause you great regret. Let everything and everyone in life be big, and you will never have to wish you could go back and undo how you treated the small things.

The Test of Truth

Zechariah 13:3

"And it shall come to pass, that when any shall yet prophesy, then his father and his mother that begat him shall say unto him, Thou shalt not live; for thou speakest lies in the name of the LORD: and his father and his mother that begat him shall thrust him through when he prophesieth."

The convicting power of truth is amazing. Zechariah prophesied that one would prophesy truth, but his parents would turn them in to be killed by the authorities. This shows the convicting power of truth, but it also shows the degree a person must take to stand for truth.

Truth is polarizing. You find throughout history that many performed horrible acts to those who proclaimed and stood for truth. Herod had John the Baptist beheaded because he told him the truth about his affair with is brother's wife. Darius had Daniel thrown into the lions den because he would not stop praying to the God of Heaven. Jeremiah was thrown into a pit because he prophesied truth. Jesus was crucified because He told the truth that He was the Son of God. Truth is certainly a dividing factor.

We live in times when people want everyone to just get along. The problem is that when truth is proclaimed there will be division. Jesus said that truth would divide in Luke 12:51 when He said, *"Suppose ye that I am come to give peace on earth? I tell you, Nay; but rather division:"* Jesus understood that there would be divisions, even among those who call themselves Christians.

How deep will these divisions go because of truth? Jesus told us in Luke 12:53, *"The father shall be divided against the son, and the son against the father; the mother against the daughter, and the daughter against the mother; the mother in law against her daughter in law, and the daughter in law against her mother in law."* Jesus said that truth would literally divide families. Children would turn against their parents and parents would turn against their children all because of truth.

Christian, the test of truth in your life is determined by what degree it takes for you to compromise. If a little fighting between Christian brethren causes you to compromise truth, your love for truth is anemic. Not only is it anemic, but your belief in truth is not really a belief at all. It is only a convenience if battles cause you to compromise truth.

Let me ask you, what will it take for you to turn on truth? If you must lose your family for the sake of truth, will you hold onto truth and lose the love of your family? If you must lose friends of a lifetime for the sake of truth, will you hold onto truth? If you must pack your bags and leave a church you attended your whole life because they compromised truth, are you willing to do it? If your alma mater teaches false doctrine, are you truly willing to stand against it for the sake of truth?

You must consider how much you truly believe in truth. I challenge you to know what the Scriptures truly teach. You will never stand for truth if you don't know what the Scriptures teach. Second, I encourage you to daily ask God to give you the courage to stand for truth when you must. Only God can give that courage. None of us know when that day will come when we must stand for truth alone, but it will come. My prayer is that you will love truth so much that no matter the cost, you will stand with truth.

Presenting Gifts to God

Matthew 2:11

"And when they were come into the house, they saw the young child with Mary his mother, and fell down, and worshipped him: and when they had opened their treasures, they presented unto him gifts; gold, and frankincense, and myrrh."

The birth of Jesus Christ is no doubt the best known story around the world. It would be hard to go to a place and find someone who has not heard of the birth of Jesus Christ. One of the events of His birth were the gifts the wise men presented to Christ. Many look at these wise men as men of wealth, but the Scriptures don't tell us if this is true.

One thing we know about these wise men is they came to Jesus and presented Him with three gifts. These same three gifts should be presented to Christ by every Christian. No, I'm not saying go down to the store or bank and purchase these things, but each of these gifts represent something far more valuable to God.

The first gift presented to Christ was gold. Gold is representative of our substance and material wealth. Every Christian needs to come to a point in their life where there is nothing that God cannot have. Everyone struggles in this area. There are many things we tell Christ He can have, but there are certain areas that seem to be off limits. For instance, every week Christians give their tithes and offerings to God and this is good, but if God laid on their heart to give something else of value to Him they would struggle. Let me ask you, what is it that you hold back from God? What is it that if God asked you to give it to Him you would hold back? It's not that God would ask you to give it to Him, but it's the fact that you are not willing to give it to Him. Everything we have, including our children, should be available to God if He were to ask.

The second gift these men presented was frankincense. Frankincense is representative of our service to God. Frankincense was often used in religious worship in the temple. Every Christian should offer their life as a tool for God to use in His service. There should never be a restriction on what God cannot ask you to do. You should be willing to serve God in any ministry in your church. Furthermore, you should be willing to serve God in full-time service either in your homeland or abroad as a missionary. It does not matter what your age may be, you should be willing to serve Him if He were to ask. Too often we put age restrictions on surrendering to serve God, but that is not found in the Scriptures. In whatever area God asks you to serve Him, you should be willing.

Myrrh was the third gift given to Jesus. Myrrh was an ointment used as a perfume. It represented the innermost thoughts and feelings of a Christian. Every Christian should open their heart to God. When God has your heart, He has you. I'm amazed how we are willing to open up anything to God, but not our heart. When is the last time you spent time with God and poured out your whole heart to Him? He can be trusted with your heart. Very few people should ever have access to your whole heart, but God is certainly One Who should have access to it.

Have you given these three gifts to God? I find the whole being of a person is found in these gifts. I challenge you today to give these things to God. Tell God that He can have any of these areas, and when He asks you for one don't hold it back.

And Jesus Went About

Matthew 9:35

"And Jesus went about all the cities and villages, teaching in their synagogues, and preaching the gospel of the kingdom, and healing every sickness and every disease among the people."

In the previous verse the Pharisees said about Jesus, *"He casteth out devils through the prince of the devils."* This was a bold statement that they made about Him. They were saying that He was possessed with devils. I know what my natural response would be if someone said that about me, but Jesus didn't let their attacks and criticisms stop Him from doing what He was supposed to do. Instead, the verse above says that *"Jesus went about all the cities and villages, teaching in their synagogues, and preaching the gospel of the kingdom..."* Instead of stopping to defend Himself or to get in a tit-for-tat squabble with the Pharisees, Jesus kept on doing what He was supposed to do.

You will find as you serve the LORD that the Devil will use many tactics to get you off track. One of the main tactics he uses to sidetrack you is to have people throw criticisms and attacks your direction. He knows that our natural reaction is to defend ourselves. Nobody likes it when they are falsely accused, but you must not let their criticisms and attacks sidetrack you from what you are supposed to do.

When criticisms and attacks come your direction, you must realize that you are making an impact. The enemy is not concerned with those who are not making an impact. They are concerned with those who are harming their sinful ways. If you were not making an impact, the Devil would leave you alone. Always remind yourself when criticisms and attacks come your way that apparently you are making a difference because the Devil would not be concerned with you if your work had no influence. Knowing you're making a difference can certainly comfort you during times of criticisms and attacks.

Moreover, when criticisms and attacks come your direction, let your works defend you. The one thing the enemy would love for you to do is to stand up and defend yourself. If you are doing what you are supposed to do, your character will defend you. This is why it's so important to make sure you are improving your character on a daily basis because you never know when you will need it in times of criticisms and attacks.

Furthermore, stay focused on what brought the criticisms and attacks. If what you were doing caused the enemy to feel that you are making an impact, the best thing you can do is to stay on course and don't stop what's making the impact. The whole reason they throw criticisms and attacks your way is to sidetrack you from what you are doing. It's so tempting to stop and fight the enemy when you are being criticized and attacked, but you cannot get off focus from the LORD's work.

Finally, always remember that time will reveal that you were right if you're doing right. We know today that Jesus was right, but time had to reveal it. Time is a great vindicator. If you will keep doing what you are supposed to do, time will show who was right and who was wrong. As hard as it is to wait for time to vindicate, you must keep doing right realizing you will eventually be vindicated.

Christian, the Devil is going to level attacks and criticisms your direction. Don't let them sidetrack you from helping people, soul winning, standing for truth and doing right. Keep doing what you are supposed to do and you will find that the LORD will reveal to all that you were right.

IMPACTING INTERACTIONS

Matthew 21:28

"But what think ye? A certain man had two sons; and he came to the first, and said, Son, go work to day in my vineyard."

Jesus told a parable about a man who had two sons. One day this man called his two sons and told them to go work in the vineyard. One son told his dad he was not going to work in the vineyard, but later he repented of his response and went and worked in the vineyard. The other son seemed to respond correctly to his father's command. He told his father that he would go, but we find that this son did not go. In this parable we find there are three interactions that will impact your life on a daily basis.

Attitude is the first impacting interaction. When you look at both of these sons, they both had two different attitudes. The first son had an attitude of rebellion and stubbornness, while the other son had an attitude of pleasing his father. We could spend pages on talking about different attitudes, but I want you to understand that your attitude will impact your life.

Your attitude to commands is imperative to how God uses you. I have found many Christians have the attitude that nobody is going to tell them what to do. This is the wrong attitude. I have heard some pride themselves in having a "little" rebelliousness inside. Having a rebellious attitude is nothing to be proud about, for rebellion is compared to witchcraft and idolatry in the Scriptures. You need to make sure you always have a right attitude when someone asks you to do something.

Answers are the second impacting interaction. There were two answers from these sons; one responded in a negative manner while the other responded in a right manner. Sometimes you can give the right answer, but give it in the wrong tone. I have often told people that you need to listen to yourself when you answer people. I know there have been times when my answer was not wrong, but the tone in my answer was wrong. People don't always know your heart. The only thing they can do is respond to your answer and the tone of it. Always make sure that you not only answer properly, but that you answer in the proper tone.

Actions are the third impacting interaction. It's interesting how the one son who had the right attitude and answer ended up having the wrong action, while the one who had the wrong attitude and answer had the right action. Following through on what you say you will do is a very important part of your credibility. If you say you are going to do something, you better make sure you do it. Many people have great intentions of doing something, but their follow through is anemic. Your actions always speak louder than your words. If you don't follow through on what you say you will do, you will find that people will lose confidence in you and will become frustrated to the point that they will stop depending on you.

All three of these interaction will impact your life. Each interaction can make or break your influence on someone's life. As a Christian, you need to be sure that all three of these interactions are performed in a right manner. Both of these sons were right at one point, but they were wrong in another. The purpose of God teaching this parable was so that we could get all three of these areas right in our lives so that we can have the greatest impact on those whom we lead and on those who depend on us.

This Is Jesus

Matthew 27:37

"And set up over his head his accusation written, THIS IS JESUS THE KING OF THE JEWS."

When Jesus was crucified, they nailed a sign over his head that said, *"THIS IS JESUS THE KING OF THE JEWS."* This sign was not written to honor Him. It was written in a derogatory manner. These people hated Jesus. They wanted to shame Him in His final moments of life. He had hurt their power over the people with His teachings. Now, they wanted to put what they thought was the final nail in His ministry so that all who saw it would never attempt it again. Though they tried to stop His ministry, we know that they failed, and the ministry of Jesus Christ still goes on today.

Though this writing was meant in a derogatory manner, they were right in what they wrote. You will notice that I put emphasis on the word "is." They wanted to make a statement that Jesus was a mere man who made the mistake of challenging their authority, but this Jesus is far more than a mere man. Think with me for a moment as I try to remind you who this Jesus is.

One may ask, "Who is this Jesus?" This Jesus is the Creator of the Universe. Though these people thought they had the power to destroy Him, they didn't understand that He was not just a mere human, but He was the One Who gave them life.

Who is this Jesus? This Jesus is the Son of God. He didn't just become the Son of God as some would like us to believe, but He **is** the Son of God and has always been the Son of God. He was not the son of Joseph, but He is the Son of God. He was born of a virgin, and not just a young lady. He was virgin born because the Holy Spirit placed the seed inside the womb of Mary. Yes, she was a sinful human, but Jesus Christ is the virgin-born, sinless Son of God.

Who is this Jesus? He is the sacrifice for sin. These people thought they killed Jesus, but that is the furthest from the truth. Jesus laid down His life so that their sins could be paid. Yes, He is the sacrificial lamb whose blood is applied upon the mercy seat in Heaven so that we have a way to have our sins atoned. It is only through the blood of this Jesus that anyone's sins can be paid.

Who is this Jesus? He is the first begotten of the dead. He is the first One Who conquered death in His own power. Others before Him who were raised from the dead did not overcome death in their power, but they overcame death through His power. This Jesus is the only One Who has the power over death so that those who trust Him can be part of the resurrection at His coming.

Who is this Jesus? He is the King of the Jews. He is the coming King Who will one day rule the world. He is the King that will come riding on a white horse to conquer the world and the world system. When He reigns, there will be peace on Earth for He is the Prince of Peace Who will conquer Satan once and for all.

Who is this Jesus? He is the Saviour of the world. Don't ever forget this! Nobody else or nothing else can save anyone from their sins. Only this Jesus can save people from their sins. Not the priest, Pope, Rabbi, pastor, or religious leader, only this Jesus can save people from their sins.

Friend, if you are saved, this Jesus is your Saviour. Don't ever take for granted Who lives within your soul. You have this Jesus living in your heart. I challenge you to boldly tell everyone who this Jesus is. Don't let the heathen shame you into silence. Around you are people who need this Jesus as their Saviour. Tell them Who He is so they can also have the opportunity to make Him their Saviour.

Shining Your Light

Mark 4:21

"And he said unto them, Is a candle brought to be put under a bushel, or under a bed? and not to be set on a candlestick?"

When the power goes out in your house, immediately the scramble starts to find the closet or drawers where you've stored your candles. You light the candles and strategically place them in positions that will give the most light to the house. The purpose for lighting and placing the candles where they are is so that everyone in the house can see in the darkness.

Imagine the power going down, and you go to the drawer to get a candle to light. Once you light the candle, you find a bushel basket and place the candle under that basket. Some in the house would wonder why you are hiding the light, for that light could be used to help everyone in the house to see. Your response to those who are clamoring for the light is that it's not your gift to let the candle light burn so all can have light. Maybe your response is that you are too afraid for people to see the light you've lighted. Maybe you are embarrassed to let others see your light because your candle isn't what they expected. All of these excuses would be foolish because you have the light that those in the house need.

God says in Matthew 5:14, *"Ye are the light of the world."* Inside of every Christian is the light of God that the world needs to get out of the darkness of sin. God reminds us how foolish it would be not to share our light by saying, *"Is a candle brought to be put under a bushel, or under a bed? and not to be set on a candlestick?"* The light inside of you was not placed there for you to hide, but it was placed there for you to shine to the world.

Christian, you must realize that the world is in darkness. Just like you are seeking a candle to light in your house when the power goes out, the world is seeking for a light to help them see in their dark world. You must not let the Devil trick you into believing that the world does not want to see the light. They do! They are in darkness, and many are seeking for someone like you to shine the light.

Moreover, it doesn't matter how old the candle is, or how fancy the candle may be, the world simply needs the light. Friend, you may think you are not the best candle to shine the light, but you must realize that the light is needed, and you have the light shining inside of you. You may not be the best deliverer of the light, but as long as the light is lit inside of you, the light will shine by itself. All you need to do is tell people about Jesus, and He will make sure the light shines.

Furthermore, don't let your foolish excuses keep you from letting your light shine. Hiding your light under the bushel of fear is only keeping people from having the answer to their darkness. You must do what you can to make sure your light brightly shines. Sin, selfishness and carelessness will dim the light that needs to shine. Make sure you remove these things from your life so that your light can brightly shine.

The world is living in darkness. They were born in a power failure, and one glimpse of the light can certainly help them to see what they are missing. I encourage you to let your light shine. Shine your light to every person whose path you come across for all they need is for someone to show them the light. Yes, some will reject the light, but move on and find those who are searching for a light. In your pathway today will be someone seeking for the light. Be sure that you shine your light by telling them about the Light of the word, Jesus Christ. Someone is waiting for you to tell them how to get out of the darkness of sin. Don't hide your light, but let it brightly shine and ask God to lead you to that one who is seeking the Light.

One Flesh

Mark 10:8

"And they twain shall be one flesh: so then they are no more twain, but one flesh."

There is much to be learned about marriage in Mark 10:6-9. Jesus had been asked if it was lawful for a couple to get divorced. To answer their question, Jesus went back to the very beginning to explain marriage and what will destroy a marriage. Let me point out several tips from this passage on helping a couple to stay married.

First, you must understand God's order in the home. Verse 6 shows us that God created man and woman. You will notice that man was created first, then the woman was created second for the man. Though this goes against modern philosophy, we must understand that the husband must be the head of the home. It does not mean the wife is a second-rate being, but simply that she was created for the man. In other words, the man cannot be what God wants him to be without his wife helping him. That means the wife has extreme influence in the marriage, but she must yield to her husband's leadership to make the marriage work.

Second, married couples must leave their parents and cleave to each other. Verse 7 shows its importance. I find this is one of the major problems in homes today. We have couples who still do everything with their parents, and this is to the detriment of their marriage. You should honor your parents, but you must cleave to your spouse. You cannot allow your parents to interfere in your home. For instance, I believe it's not good to have a vacation with your parents every year. Every once in awhile is not bad, but not every year. You must leave your parents and cleave to your spouse. Your family needs to spend the vacation together so that it can create its own memories.

Third, you must become one in all that you do. This will only happen if you spend time with each other. You cannot have one process of thinking if you don't know each other. May I encourage you to make time to be with each other. Don't get so wrapped up in hobbies, career, ministry, making money and other activities that you are never home to spend time with each other. If your marriage is going to make it, you and your spouse need to spend time together to be one in all that you do.

Fourth, don't let any person divide your marriage. God warns that people will divide your marriage. This subject alone could take up many pages, but let me try to simplify it by saying that no person should come between you and your spouse. Your children or parents should not come between you and your spouse. Definitely, no person of the opposite gender should come between you. Also, be careful that other authorities don't come between you. Always be aware that these will destroy a marriage.

Finally, hardened hearts are the greatest destroyer of marriages. You will notice that Jesus said, *"For the hardness of your heart he wrote you this precept."* Be careful that you don't have a heart that nobody can change. When you get the type of spirit in your marriage that your spouse is not going to change you, then you have started down a destructive path. Couples who stay together must be tender towards each other. Hard hearts cause strife and divisions in the marriage. Don't always have to have things your way. Be agreeable with each other and don't let anything harden your heart towards your spouse.

If you will take these precepts and apply them to your marriage, you will find your marriage will become stronger. Though I could not go in depth into these precepts, you must see the importance of these things in your marriage. Marriage is a work in progress, and each of these areas must be worked on continually if you want to stay happily married.

Fixing the Broken

Luke 4:18

"The Spirit of the Lord is upon me, because he hath anointed me to preach the gospel to the poor; he hath sent me to heal the brokenhearted, to preach deliverance to the captives, and recovering of sight to the blind, to set at liberty them that are bruised,"

You will notice that everyone whom Jesus went after were in some way or another broken. It is interesting the Jesus didn't go to those who had everything together, but only to those who seemed to be living a life of hopelessness. His whole ministry was about trying to fix the broken.

Look at those whom Jesus went after. He went after the poor to give them the good news that they can be rich in spirit. He sought the brokenhearted to give them hope to heal their wounds. He worked to help those who had been held captive by sin. He helped those who were blinded by life, and he found those who were for some reason bruised in life and gave them the hope that they could be freed from the bruise of sin. What a fulfilling ministry Jesus had in trying to fix the broken.

We would be wise to pattern our ministries after Jesus. Instead of trying to find those who have it all together, we would be wise to find those who truly need help. I have watched pastors and church members alike get excited when someone who seems to have everything together joins their church. Yet, you never hear people get excited when someone joins the church whose life seems to be in ruins.

Friend, let me remind you that a good church is not a museum where we praise the people who are so "great," but church is an emergency room full of Christians trying to fix those who are broken in life. Yes, those who are broken certainly bring their problems with them, but the joy of seeing a life turned around is exciting and fulfilling. If a church is going to be what God wants it to be, they will go after the broken.

Moreover, let me also remind you that when you go after the broken you will have to deal with their baggage of sin. When you bring in the broken, you will have to help put their life back together. As a Christian, we must not fall for Satan's trap of looking down on those who are broken. We must remember that many of us were there at one point ourselves, and if we are honest with ourselves, we still have areas in our own life that are broken. Don't bemoan those coming into the church who have broken lives, for that is what God wants His church to go after.

Furthermore, you will find that God's power comes to those who seek the broken. The verse above says, *"The Spirit of the Lord is upon me, because he hath anointed me to..."* God's power does not fall on those who are seeking to fill their church with those who have no problems, but He fills the Christian who tries to fix the broken with power to help those who are broken.

Christian, the church that God is interested in is the church that is actively pursuing the broken. If your church is not actively pursuing the broken, I would reconsider where you attend. You want to be in a church that God is interested in, and that church is the church that is an emergency room that is open to fix those who are broken.

Focus

Luke 9:51

"And it came to pass, when the time was come that he should be received up, he stedfastly set his face to go to Jerusalem,"

One of the main ingredients to the success of the earthly ministry of Jesus Christ was that He was focused. It says in the verse above, *"...he steadfastly set his face to go to Jerusalem,"* What was so special about going to Jerusalem? It was that He knew He would die for the sins of the world in Jerusalem. That was the whole reason He came to Earth, and that was why He was focused.

The word "focus" means, the center of interest or activity. In other words, everything Jesus did centered around Him dying on the cross for the sins of the world. If something came His direction that would have been a good thing to do but it wouldn't center around Him paying for our sins, He would not get involved. The focus of our Saviour is one of the main reasons He succeeded in His earthly ministry, and the main reason you and I can go to Heaven.

A person without focus is a person who is going nowhere. When I ran track in high school, we were trained to keep our eyes on the finish line. We were to be focused on where we were going. We were told that if we turned our head that we would get of course. Over and over again we were drilled about staying focused on the finish line. The finish line was where we were going.

Are you truly focused on what God wants you to do? A preacher who is not focused on his calling is a preacher who will one day find himself out of the ministry. A Christian who is not focused on winning souls will find themselves involved in activities that are meaningless. A church that is not focused is a church that will start useless ministries that have nothing to do with winning the lost to Jesus Christ.

Friend, focus is the key to keeping sin from ruining your life. When you get focused on what God wants you to do, you will find that sin's lure will not be great. One of the biggest reasons people step into sin is because they lose their focus. It's not that they are bad people, they simply lost focus. Saul lost his focus and went into sin. David lost his focus and committed adultery. Samson lost his focus and hobnobbed with the enemy. If you don't want sin to ruin your life, you need to stay focused on the souls of men.

Christian, be careful that you don't allow the noise of the world to distract you from your focus. Keep your eye on what you are supposed to do. Don't let your trials cause you to lose focus. When going through trials it is easy to lose focus of why God has left you on this Earth, but you must continue to stay focused on the souls of men. Furthermore, you must not let good things pull you away from your focus. There are many things with which you can involve yourself, but you must never allow yourself to be involved with things that pull you away from your focus.

The best way to look at this is to look at a bicycle wheel. Your focus is the hub of the wheel, and every spoke comes from that hub. Everything you do must come from the hub or the focus of your life. If what you do is not attached to the hub, you are losing focus. Regularly look at everything you do and make sure that you are not losing focus. Be sure that everything you do is connected to the hub of reaching the lost for Jesus Christ. That should be your focus in life. Staying focused will not be easy, but if it is achieved it will help you to succeed as a Christian.

Getting Along with Others

Luke 17:3

"Take heed to yourselves: If thy brother trespass against thee, rebuke him; and if he repent, forgive him."

Getting along with others is not always an easy task. Differences in personalities, opinions, and techniques make getting along with others one of the hardest things a person will do and especially with those we interact with on a daily basis. Jesus taught the disciples a lesson on how to get along with others, and He gave them six things they must do to accomplish this.

First, be careful with how you treat people. The very first thing that Jesus said to the disciples was, *"Take heed to yourselves..."* Jesus was trying to get the disciples to learn to look at their own actions before looking at the actions of others. I have always found that I will have an easier time getting along with others if I will look at what I can correct in myself instead of looking at how to correct them. The biggest problem you have is not someone else, it is you. This first key is imperative to getting along with everyone.

Second, don't always assume others did wrong. Again, *"Take heed to yourselves..."* In other words, if you look at your own actions before accusing others, you will find yourself having an easier time getting along. When a wrong has happened, immediately assume that you did the wrong instead of accusing someone else. You will have a hard time getting along with others if you always assume they were in the wrong.

Third, don't assume you know the intentions of others. When you take heed to yourself, you will stop assuming others intentions. It is so easy to fall into the trap of judging the intentions of others, but you don't know their intentions, so stop trying to judge why another person did something. Believe in the good of people instead of the bad.

Fourth, correct with an attitude to forgive. Even when you must correct someone, you must do so with an intent to forgive. The key to the verse above is forgiveness. If your correction is given with no intention to forgive, then your correction will cause strife.

Fifth, don't put a limit on forgiveness. One of the most important things you can do is never give up on people. This is why you must not put a limit on forgiveness. Aren't you glad God doesn't put a limit on how many times He will forgive you? You must not put a limit on how many times you will forgive another. Forgiveness is a belief that they will do better. Always believe that others will turn their actions around, and you will find it will not be hard to forgive.

Sixth, don't hold people to your expectations. The word *"trespass"* means to miss the mark. In other words, if you're going to get along with another, when they miss the mark that you have set for them you must be willing to forgive. I have found the best way to accomplish this is not to expect others to live according to my expectations. My expectations are selfish and are not the measuring stick by which others should be measured. God set the measuring stick by which we should live, so stop trying to force others to live according to your expectations.

These six principles are important to getting along with others. Whether it is in your marriage, home, church, workplace or surroundings, these six principles will help you to get along with others. Don't be a person with whom it is hard to get along. Life is too short to constantly being at odds with others, so work at getting along.

Enhancing Your Life

1 Corinthians 1:5

"That in every thing ye are enriched by him, in all utterance, and in all knowledge;"

One of the main reasons the church of Corinth was so fleshly was because they took their eyes off God and placed them on man. Paul starts his discourse with this church in this verse to show them exactly where they failed. He said to them, *"That in every thing ye are enriched by him..."* The reason they allowed fleshly sins in the church was because they took their eyes off Christ. When they took their eyes off Christ, they lost the benefit of being *"enriched by him."*

The word *"enriched"* means to be enhanced or to be made wealthy. Paul was not talking about them being made wealthy financially; he was talking about their spiritual life being wealthy. Instead, this church was spiritually poor. Why were they spiritually poor? Because they took their eyes of Christ and lost His help to enhance their life. Yet, Paul said that through Christ we are *"enriched"* in every thing.

First, you will notice that Christ will help enhance your speech. I know right now the "educated" people look at this and think this is foolish, but God's Word said that Christ will enrich them *"in all utterance."* When you keep your eyes on Christ, you will find that He will guide your conversations. It is interesting to watch a person's conversation change when they spend much time in the Scriptures. When you spend time with Christ, He changes your language.

One of the greatest illustrations of this is the Apostle Peter. Reading through the Gospels you see that Peter had a problem with cursing, but after much time with Christ his cursing tongue was cleaned up. God always enhances your ability to speak. He will not only clean up your language, but He will also bring your standard of speaking to a higher level. You will converse on a more knowledgeable basis with Christ's help.

Second, Christ will enhance your knowledge. The verse above clearly states that Christ will enrich you *"in all knowledge."* You must realize that Christ is the source of all knowledge. Spending time with Christ makes you smarter in every area. The mechanic will have their mechanical skills enhanced by spending time with Christ. The physician will have their medical knowledge enhanced by spending time with Christ. The lawyer and judge will have their judicial knowledge enhanced by spending time with Christ. The computer technician will have their computer knowledge enhanced by spending time with Christ. The educator will have their knowledge enhanced by spending time with Christ. It doesn't matter what field you work in, if you spend time with Christ He will enhance your knowledge in that area.

Furthermore, you must remember that God says He will enrich you *"in every thing."* That means every area of life is enhanced when you spend time with Christ and keep your eyes on Him. Your marital and family life is enhanced by keeping your eyes on Christ. Your spiritual life will be enhanced by spending time with Christ. No matter what you do, Christ enhances every area of life.

Christian, don't forget to ask Christ to help you in every thing you do. When you drive down the road, ask Christ to help you. When you cook a meal, ask Christ to help you. When you study for a test, ask Christ to help you. Whatever you do, Christ will make everything you do better if you will keep your eyes on Him. The secret to making your life better is to keep your eyes on Christ.

The Greatest Kingdom to Conquer

Proverbs 25:28

"He that hath no rule over his own spirit is like a city that is broken down, and without walls."

God says that a person who does not control their own spirit is like a defenseless city. In ancient times the only way a city had to defend itself was to build a wall around its borders. You may recall that there is much written in the Scriptures about the walls of Jerusalem. Those walls were there to protect that city from outside sources. God likens a city without walls to the person who does not control their own spirit.

The greatest kingdom you will conquer in life is your own spirit. I have watched people conquer the financial kingdom, but have it destroyed because they never conquered their own spirit. I have watched people climb the ladder of success only to destroy it by not controlling their spirit. It does not matter what kingdoms you may conquer, if you don't conquer the kingdom of your spirit then you will find that every success will eventually be destroyed. There are some definite spirits you need to conquer in your life.

First, the spirit of bitterness will destroy your life. Bitterness has destroyed the best. One of the people I think of in the Scriptures who did not conquer the spirit of bitterness was Saul. He was bitter because David got more recognition than he did, and it literally destroyed his kingdom. I certainly don't pretend to know what has happened to you in your lifetime, but you must never let anything cause you to become bitter. You must learn to forgive, for forgiveness is the wall that protects you against bitterness.

Second, you need to conquer the spirit of haughtiness. Proverbs 16:18 says, *"Pride goeth before destruction, and an haughty spirit before a fall."* Many people have allowed success to go to their head only to see their haughtiness destroy them. I have watched financial success, education degrees and position cause many to become haughty. The only way to conquer the spirit of haughtiness is to stay humble before God and realize that you are truly nothing without Him.

Third, you must conquer the discouraging spirit. There are people who are negative about everything. This type of spirit will destroy your family and future. A discouraging spirit doesn't change your surroundings, but it will destroy you. The only way to conquer a discouraging spirit is to allow your joy to come from within. If you don't let outside circumstances control your spirit, then you can conquer the discouraging spirit.

Fourth, you need to conquer the know-it-all spirit. A know-it-all is truly an annoying person. It doesn't matter what you have done, the know-it-all has always done it better. At the core of the know-it-all spirit is pride. Pride causes a person to think they know more than another. Always remember that everyone knows something that you do not know, and your journey with others should be to learn from them what you do not know. The best way to conquer the know-it-all spirit is to stop looking at what you do know and look at how much you do not know.

These are just four spirits a person must conquer in life. What spirit is it that you need to conquer? Being in control of your own spirit is imperative to your future. One of your daily prayers should be to ask the Holy Spirit to control your spirit so that you don't destroy the work that God wants to do through your life. Don't live your life with broken down walls, but with God's help conquer the greatest kingdom you can conquer in life, your spirit.

Fallen From Grace

Galatians 5:4

"Christ is become of no effect unto you, whosoever of you are justified by the law; ye are fallen from grace."

What does it mean to fall from grace? Does it mean that a person can lose their salvation? Not at all! When trying to understand any portion of Scripture, you must look at all of the Scriptures to see what a phrase means. When looking at the Scriptures as a whole, you understand that once a person is saved they will always be saved. God promised to give us eternal life at salvation. If God would have promised conditional life, then we would understand that our salvation is based upon conditions that God set up. However, God said that He gave us eternal life at salvation. That means no matter what we do after salvation we will always be saved.

The word *"fallen"* means, to drop away or to be driven out of one's course. In other words, when a person falls away from grace, that means they stop living the Christian lifestyle and start living a life of sin. Verse 7 probably explains this phrase the best when it says, *"Ye did run well; who did hinder you that ye should not obey the truth?"* Notice, to fall from grace mean someone stopped obeying the truth. To fall from grace means to drop away from living the Christian life. To fall from grace means to get off course. It means something sidetracked the Christian from living the way they were supposed to live. In other words, they stopped living the Christian life to live some other lifestyle. Yes, they are still saved, but they fell away from the life that grace gave.

Christian, when you got saved, you were saved from a life of sin to a life of freedom in Christ. Why would you ever want to go back to bondage? Why would you ever think another life would give you more freedom? God saved you to live a life of freedom. His grace is given so that you no longer have to be in bondage to sin. You must be careful that nothing sidetracks you from living the Christian life.

Throughout my lifetime I have had many dogs as pets. In recent years my dogs have been trained. Whenever my dog listens to me, they earn the freedom to be off leash when we take walks in the morning. As long as the dog obeys my voice and doesn't get sidetracked from other dogs or people, it has the freedom to not be restrained by a leash. The freedom does not permit the dog to do whatever it wants, but rather to enjoy life under the guidelines that I set forth. Any time the dog stops listening to my voice, it is put back on the leash until it learns to obey the voice of its master.

As long as a Christian listens to the voice of Jesus Christ, they will experience the freedom of grace. The only thing that will cause a Christian to fall away from the graces of God is to start disobeying His voice. Whenever you leave the life of obedience to Christ, you fall away from God's grace to God's judgment.

Christian, be careful about listening to any voice that tries to pull you away from serving the LORD. Verse 7 says it was a *"who"* that hindered someone and caused them to fall away from grace. Any voice but God's voice will lead you away from God's graces. Don't let the voices of the world sidetrack you from serving God. They may seem inviting, but freedom is only experienced by obeying Christ. Keep your eyes on God and live the life He commands you to live, and in that life you will find the greatest freedom. Sin always leads to bondage, but obedience to God's voice allows the Christian to enjoy the freedom of God's grace.

Striving Together

Philippians 1:27

"Only let your conversation be as it becometh the gospel of Christ: that whether I come and see you, or else be absent, I may hear of your affairs, that ye stand fast in one spirit, with one mind striving together for the faith of the gospel;"

One of the sad things about Christians is that we tend to fight against each other more than we work together. With so many things that seem worthy of fighting for, you would think that we could set aside some of our petty differences for the sake of the Gospel. If our personality conflicts could be set aside, I truly believe that we could strive together to accomplish great things for God.

Paul challenged the church at Philippi to strive together *"for the faith of the gospel."* In the previous verses, he explains how there were many who were preaching Christ, not for the sake of the Gospel, but to add contention among the brethren and to add to his affliction. By challenging them to strive together, he was saying they needed to wrestle together or labor together for the furtherance of the Gospel. With this thought in mind, let me point out some things that God emphasized about striving together.

First, the focal point is the Gospel. I want you to notice that God does not say to strive together to get someone elected into office, to get legislation passed or to see a social agenda furthered. They were to strive together to spread the Gospel. The Gospel of Jesus Christ must always be our focal point in striving together.

Second, the challenge was to a local church. Paul was not challenging every church to strive together, but he gave the challenge to one local church. Often we take this challenge that every church needs to set aside their differences for the sake of the Gospel. NO! This is written to the local church. We must be careful that we don't get so focused on unity that we believe unity between churches is what God wants. God never addresses a conglomerate of churches. He always addresses the local church. The local church is to strive together for the Gospel.

Third, the challenge was to strive together for the Gospel and not the furtherance of a personality. One of the biggest problems I see in our churches today is that we get caught up in fighting for personalities and not for the Gospel. Let me make it clear that the only personality for Whom we are to fight is the personality of Jesus Christ. Stop striving for human personalities and start striving for the Gospel.

Fourth, we are not to compromise what we believe to strive for the Gospel. Notice that the challenge to strive was for the *"**faith** of the gospel."* I'm not to lay aside the faith so the Gospel can be spread; I'm to hold onto the faith and strive to spread the Gospel. Don't fall for the Devil's trap that we must set aside the faith so the Gospel can be spread. If you lose the faith, then you will start spreading a different gospel.

Fifth, don't get so wrapped up in striving that you turn to striving against each other. Be careful that you don't get so used to fighting that you start fighting those who are fighting with you. It's easy to get in such a fighting spirit that you get sidetracked and start fighting those along side of you. Don't fight people; fight for the faith. Yes, our opponent is always a human, but we must realize we are not fighting them, but we are fighting that for which they stand. Your goal should be to see your opponent reached with the Gospel you're striving to spread.

Friend, keep your focus right. Remember it is a battle and you will unfortunately lose people in this battle, but continue to strive together with those in your local church so the Gospel can reach the lost of your city.

The LORD's Memorial

1 Corinthians 11:24

"And when he had given thanks, he brake it, and said, Take, eat: this is my body, which is broken for you: this do in remembrance of me."

I have had the privilege of visiting several memorials in my lifetime. I have seen the Vietnam Wall Memorial in Washington D.C., the World War II memorial in the Philippines and Arlington National Cemetery. Each of these memorials commemorate the memory of people who gave their life for the freedom of their country. I could not imagine someone going to the Tomb of the Unknown Soldier and jumping on it or writing graffiti on it. This is unthinkable because these places are memorials, and memorials are to be honored.

God said that the LORD's Supper is to be done *"in remembrance of me."* Every time you take the LORD's Supper, you are remembering what He did for you on Calvary. God takes this time of remembrance seriously for it was His Son Who gave His life for the world. There are several things you should do when taking the LORD's Supper.

First, let it be a time of self-examination. Verse 28 says, *"But let a man examine himself..."* The LORD's Supper should be a time when the Christian makes sure that there is no known sin in their life. It is very dangerous to take the LORD's Supper *"unworthily."* Verses 29-30 say, *"For he that eateth and drinketh unworthily, eateth and drinketh damnation to himself, not discerning the LORD's body. For this cause many are weak and sickly among you, and many sleep."* When a person takes the LORD's Supper with known sin in their life, they are asking God to punish them. You will notice that God says those who have taken it unworthily have ended up *"weak...sickly"* and some have even died. Always take time before you take the LORD's Supper to take an honest look at yourself and be sure to get rid of sin.

Second, treat the LORD's Supper with respect. Remember, this is done in memory of what Jesus did for us on Calvary. The LORD's Supper is not a time to be talking, it should be a solemn time. It should be a time of prayer and thanksgiving. You should never take the LORD's Supper flippantly. Parents need to be sure their children understand the importance of taking the LORD's Supper and also teach them how to act during it. In fact, I believe it would be wise for parents to have their children sit next to them during this time.

Third, remember what Christ endured on Calvary. When you take the bread, remember how He allowed His body to be bruised, beaten, tortured and broken so that your sins could be paid. Remember when you drink the juice how His blood is the only blood that can atone for sin. Friend, we would not be saved without the blood of Jesus Christ. When you hold the bread or juice in your hand, always take the time to silently pray and thank Jesus Christ for coming to Earth to pay for your sin.

Finally, make the LORD's Supper a true memorial in your heart and mind. Though Jesus Christ has risen from the grave, what He did for us on Calvary must be properly and reverently remembered. It not only becomes a time of cleansing, but it also becomes a time of motivation to stir us to do more for Him. However regularly your church takes the LORD's Supper, make it such a sacred time that you would not miss it nor treat it in such a flippant manner for it is the LORD's memorial.

Treatment of the Disorderly

2 Thessalonians 3:6

"Now we command you, brethren, in the name of our Lord Jesus Christ, that ye withdraw yourselves from every brother that walketh disorderly, and not after the tradition which he received of us."

Every parent who truly cares for their child will prevent them from playing with children who could turn them away from what they are supposed to be. I remember when I was a boy there were people my age with whom when my mother would not let me spend much time. There were times my mother would not let me go to someone's birthday party because she knew that person would be a bad influence on me. She was not trying to be mean to that family, but she was simply trying to protect her son.

If a parent will protect their child from bad influences, why would God not protect His children from bad influences? In fact, He does! In the verse above, God makes it very clear that there are some bad influences with whom Christians should not associate. God was not talking about the bad influences that come from the world, but He was talking about Christian brethren who are bad influences. God calls them disorderly. Who are these bad or disorderly influences from whom we are to withdraw?

First, you are to withdraw yourself from the influences who don't properly believe the Word of God. 2 Thessalonians 2:15 says, *"Therefore, brethren, stand fast, and hold the traditions which ye have been taught, whether by word, or our epistle."* When someone does not believe the King James Bible is the Word of God, you are to withdraw from them. In other words, you don't go to their church, read their books or associate with them, for they are a disorderly influence.

Second, you are to withdraw from those who don't hold the traditions we have been taught by our forefathers. This is interesting in that God wants us to know what those before us taught. In other words, there are people who avoid being associated with those who stood in the past, but God says to withdraw from those who would be critical of them. There are men like J. Frank Norris, Lee Roberson, Jack Hyles and Tom Malone who have shown us how to build a church and separate from liberals. Instead of being critical of their methods, God says to withdraw from those who are critical of their methods.

Third, withdraw yourself from those who won't work. Verse 10 shows us that not working is a disorderly influence. In other words, those who are lazy both in the spiritual and earthly realm should be avoided. Don't go to churches that are not aggressively going after the lost. Lazy churches and lazy Christians should be avoided. Likewise, those who don't physically work are people from whom you should withdraw. God doesn't want you to learn their disorderly ways.

What is interesting is that God says in verses 14-15, *"And if any man obey not our word by this epistle, note that man, and have no company with him, that he may be ashamed. Yet count him not as an enemy, but admonish him as a brother."* Notice that you are not to be unfriendly to these people, but you are to be kind and treat them *"as a brother"* when you are around them. God is not saying that we have to be a jerk to these people. We are to be kind to them when we see them, but just don't spend time with them.

God is interested in your spiritual well-being. God telling you to withdraw from someone should not be grievous to you, but it should be a sense of endearment that God cares enough about you to protect you from disorderly influences. Don't let the disorderly make you feel bad because you withdraw. God says in verse 13, *"…be not weary in well doing."* It won't be easy to withdraw, but God knows it is best for you if you want to serve Him with your entire life.

Protecting Your Influence

1 Timothy 4:16

"Take heed unto thyself, and unto the doctrine; continue in them: for in doing this thou shalt both save thyself, and them that hear thee."

Influence is defined as the capacity to have an effect on the character, development, or behavior of someone. Everyone has influence on someone, and nobody knows the amount of influence they have. Sadly, you never learn someone's influence until they do something wrong or they pass away; however, the fingers of influence always go deeper than anyone can imagine.

The Apostle Paul cautioned young Timothy about his influence. What is interesting in his caution about influence is that Paul said that we not only influence others, but we also influence ourselves. In his caution to Timothy about influence, he tells him that there are three areas in which he must be extremely careful to protect his influence from becoming a wrong influence.

First, Paul cautioned Timothy to be careful how he lived. He says, *"Take heed unto thyself..."* How you live will influence what you become and what you lead others to do. One of the common statements I make is that you must always think about the next generation with every decision you make. The way you live may not cause you to go into sin or compromise truth, but it may cause the next generation who follows you to sin or compromise.

You must realize that someone is watching you all the time. When you think you are alone, someone is still watching. Moreover, even if nobody were watching you, what you do in your private life is influencing you to become something in the future. You must be very careful with how you live so that your influence will not lead others down the wrong way.

Second, Paul cautioned Timothy to be careful with what he believed. He says, *"Take heed...unto the doctrine..."* Many people have doctrinally changed throughout the years and influenced others to go down a wrong path. Friend, be careful whom and what you read. Let the Word of God be your final authority on everything. If you read a book that presents something new, don't immediately jump on the bandwagon until you study the Scriptures. I like what one preacher told me years ago, he said if you hear something that causes you to raise an eyebrow, then you're probably listening to something that raises God's eyebrow.

Third, Paul cautioned Timothy to be faithful. He says, "...*continue in them...*" Your faithfulness to what you believe and to living what you believe is imperative to your influence. To say you believe something and to live a life contrary to that belief, only influences people to copy what you live. People will always follow your last act. You must be careful that your last act won't influence someone to do wrong.

Christian, don't ever forget that you have an influence on someone. These three areas where Paul cautioned Timothy are critical to protecting your influence. Don't let your influence lead someone to do wrong, but let your influence be positive for the sake of Christ. Always remember that everything you do is your last act, and people will always follow your last act.

Missing Out on God's Blessings

Hebrews 3:12

"Take heed, brethren, lest there be in any of you an evil heart of unbelief, in departing from the living God."

The children of Israel missed out on the greatest blessings of God because they would not by faith obey God's command to go into the Promised Land. For forty years they wandered, complained, murmured and many died because they doubted what God said He would do through them. It is sad that they missed out on forty years of God's blessings. We will never know what blessings God had for them had they obeyed and went forward into the Promised Land.

It is sad to say that most of us miss out of God's blessings just like the children of Israel. It is easy to sit in judgment as we look back at them and understand that God did come through and brought them into the Promised Land, but God also has a Promised Land for us and we must claim it by faith or else we also will miss out on God's blessings. God shows us in Hebrews 3 the one step a person takes that causes them to miss out on His blessings.

The one step they took was not believing God's promise. Notice it says in the verse above, *"lest there be in any of you an evil heart of unbelief..."* What kept the children of Israel from going into the Promised Land? Unbelief! It wasn't the giants of the land that kept them from experiencing God's blessings. It wasn't the huge walls that prevented them from enjoying God's blessings. It wasn't the iron chariots that hindered God's blessings. Though these were their excuses, the actual reason they missed out on God's blessings was because they didn't believe God.

What are the excuses you have used to disobey the will of God? In God's will are His blessings. If you choose to use an excuse to camouflage your unbelief, you are choosing not to have God's blessings on your life. Your unbelief in God's Word is the only thing preventing you from His blessings.

A person's unbelief that God will bless them if they will tithe is the only thing keeping them from His blessings. The unbelief that God could use you to win someone to Christ is the only thing keeping you from His blessings. The unbelief that prevents you from going forward into God's will for your life is the only thing keeping you from experiencing His blessings.

Friend, God's blessings will only be experienced when you live the life of faith and obey. The Book of Hebrews is all about living the life of faith, and the children of Israel missed out on God's blessings because of their lack of faith. Verse 19 says, *"So we see that they could not enter in because of unbelief."*

I ask you, what is preventing you from entering your Promised Land? Always remember that the reason you are not experiencing God's blessings is never His fault; it is yours. Unbelief in what God tells us to do is what turns off His blessings.

I encourage you to always obey God's voice. I know at times you may not see how it will work, but you always have to obey God to receive His blessings. There have been many times in my life when God wanted me to do something and it seemed impossible, but every time I obeyed I received His blessings. Likewise, God's blessings are waiting for you, but you must plug your ears to the voice of unbelief and step out by faith and obey God. When you do this, you will see God's blessings begin to pour out on your life.

Provoking Family Relationships

Hebrews 10:24

"And let us consider one another to provoke unto love and to good works:"

The family relationship and the relationship of the Christian and the church mirror each other. For instance, you show me what type of relationship you have with your spouse and I will show you what type of relationship you have with God. They are a mirror of each other. You show me what type of relationship a Christian has with their church and I will show you what type of relationship a person has with their family. You cannot separate them because one affects the other.

In the verse above, we are commanded to provoke each other. The word *"provoke"* means, to stimulate, to call into action or to give rise to an emotion. God was showing the Christian what it would take to keep a good relationship with Him and the church. These same actions are needed to provoke strong family relationships.

First, to provoke love in the family, each member of the family must be filled with good works. When family members become selfish and make everything about themselves, instead of having a family filled with love you will have a family filled with selfishness. You will never have a strong family without each person in the family working to help each other. This is why I believe it's important that the children get involved in helping their parents around the house. It teaches them to be filled with good works so that love prevails in the family.

Second, if you are going to have strong family relationships, then you must have time together. Verse 25 says, *"Not forsaking the assembling of ourselves together..."* God is showing the Christian the importance of church attendance and their relationship with other brothers and sisters. If it is important for

Christians to assemble together to keep a strong relationship with their church, then it's important for families to have time with each other.

There are some times I believe that are important for families to assemble with each other. Every family should assemble to have their evening meal together. If at all possible, I believe it would be good to have breakfast together as well. These are times to talk about your day. Furthermore, I also believe you should have daily family devotions. This will provoke spirituality in the family. Moreover, I also believe it's important to have a family vacation together. This will help the family to enjoy time away from everyone else to build ties together.

Third, strong family relationships are built by exhorting each other. Verse 25 says, "...but exhorting one another..." The family must not be a place where they compete against each other for superiority, but it should be a place where they cheer for every member's success. Don't let your family be a place where each member is tearing the other down, but make your family a place where encouragement is present. Every member of the family should know that they at least have their family in their corner.

Friend, you only have one family. I encourage you to strengthen your family. Let your home be a place that is filled with love, encouragement and spirituality. A home that has an atmosphere filled with these things is a home where you will find joy and close bonds.

Pleasant Places

Psalm 16:6

"The lines are fallen unto me in pleasant places; yea, I have a goodly heritage."

In my lifetime I have had the privilege of going to some very exotic places. My wife and I have had the privilege of going to Hawaii, a place that we both extremely enjoyed and hope to go back to someday. We have enjoyed going to the Caribbean and seeing some of the beautiful sights there. We have been in the majestic mountains of the United States and enjoyed their grandeur. All of these places I reminisce as pleasant places.

In this psalm, David did not bemoan the fact of who he was and from whence he came. He called the heritage of God a pleasant place and *"goodly."* In other words, he looked at his heritage as a place to which he enjoyed going. He looked at his heritage as something of considerable size. It was something of which he was proud.

When we think of what God has done for us, it should be like the pleasant places you go to in your mind; places of enjoyment. I'm afraid there are many who look at the heritage of the LORD as unpleasant places. I find in our day there are many who want to run away from the pleasant places of God's heritage when we should be running to our heritage and understand that God's heritage is what has given us many of the blessings we enjoy today. In this psalm we can see many of the things God's heritage does for us.

First, God's heritage instructs us. Verse 7 says, *"I will bless the LORD, who hath given me counsel: my reins also instruct me in the night seasons."* If you will not despise the heritage of the LORD, you will find all the counsel you need. Christians don't need to be running to the unproven methods of modern preachers, instead they need to go to their heritage and let the lessons of the old-time Christians counsel them on what they should do. God's heritage is the greatest counselor for your life if you will learn to run to it and learn from it.

Second, God's heritage protects and establishes you. Verse 8 says, *"because he is at my right hand, I shall not be moved."* You will find when you live in the heritage God has given you that He will protect you from heartache. Far too many Christians run from God's lifestyle only to find themselves in heartache and ruin. If you will live in God's prescribed lifestyle, you will find that He will protect you as you get established in life.

Third, God's heritage gives you hope for the future. Verse 9 talks about the hope God's heritage gives. Why does it give hope? Because in verse 11 it shows us the path to take in life. I have found that if I will stay in God's heritage, God guides me even when I'm not asking for His guidance. I'm amazed how God has protected me from much heartache all because I have lived in the pleasant place of God's heritage. Because of this, it gives me hope that my future is bright. You can have that same hope for your future if you will let God's heritage guide your life.

Friend, the heritage of God is found in the pages of the Word of God. Study God's Word and live how it tells you to live. Study the old-time Christians, and instead of criticizing them for how strict they are, embrace them for they are a part of your heritage. When you look at what God's heritage can do for you, you can't help but agree with David that His heritage is a pleasant place to live.

This is the Love of God

1 John 5:3

"For this is the love of God, that we keep his commandments: and his commandments are not grievous."

One of the biggest criticisms that I receive is that I need to preach more about the love of God than about the "do's" and "don'ts" of the Scriptures. Those who are critical of me would say that my type of preaching is hateful and legalistic. Their criticism is that preaching that exposes sin will not reach those who are lost.

Yet, what is the love of God? If you were to ask the critics, they would say that the love of God is that God loves us no matter what we do, and they are right. They would say that the love of God is that Jesus came to Earth to die for man's sins, and they are right. Certainly, God's love is revealed in these acts.

However, who better to define the love of God than God Himself? In the verse above, God shows us the definition of His love. He says, *"For this is the love of God, that we keep his commandments..."* This is interesting, because most people would never say that this is the love of God. This means that someone must tell us His commandments so we can keep them. If the love of God is to keep His commandments, then we must know what they are so we can show His love to the world.

Let me explain why God's commandments are the love of God. I would not be much of a parent if I didn't tell my daughter what would hurt her in life. If all I do is to tell my daughter I love her, but don't tell her what would damage her future or destroy her life, then my love would be suspect. Because I love my daughter, I have told her that drugs are bad, alcohol is a sin, lying is not permitted, cheating will bring punishment, etc. All of these things will bring hurtful results in her life. Because I love her, I tell her what is wrong to keep her from hurt. My commandments for my daughter show my love because they keep her from being hurt.

God is called our Father. If He is our Father, then He must teach us what we can and cannot do to keep us from hurting ourselves. In fact, verse 4 shows us that He gives us His commandments so that we can overcome the world. God, in His love, gave us His Word that is filled with commandments by which to live so that we can overcome the world. His love must reveal His commandments to keep us from hurting ourselves.

I contend that those who don't teach and preach the commandments of God are those who truly don't want you to know God's love. God's commandments are not grievous to those who obey them because we know what they have kept us from doing. Don't criticize the preacher who is very precise about God's commandments, for he is only revealing to you God's love. The preacher with whom you should be upset is the preacher who does not teach you God's commandments, for he is hiding God's love from you.

Let me take this thought one step further. Not only is God's love revealed in His commandments, but our love for God is revealed in what we think of His commandments and what we do with them. If God's commandments are grievous to us, then our love for God is shallow. If I love God, then I will keep His commandments as John 14:15 says, *"If ye love me, keep my commandments."*

Let me ask you, how much do you love God and His love for you? If you complain about people teaching you God's commandments, then you don't want God's love. If you don't live His commandments, then you don't love God. God's commandments reveal His love for you because He not only wants to save you from Hell, but He shows you how to live to save you from the world.

It Only Takes a Few

Revelation 3:4

"Thou hast a few names even in Sardis which have not defiled their garments; and they shall walk with me in white: for they are worthy."

The church of Sardis was one of seven churches that God addressed. The church was located in the metropolis of Lydia in Asia Minor. This church had apparently lost its zeal to reach the lost for Christ. God said in verse 1, *"I know thy works, that thou hast a name that thou livest, and art dead."*

We don't know, but this church could have been a larger church because everyone thought they were a church that was alive, but God knew they were dying. The works this church used to produce they were no longer producing. The standards this church used to have were gone because they had succumbed to the pressures of their society. God says concerning this in the verse above that there were a few who had *"not defiled their garments."* That would mean there were many who had defiled their spiritual garments and started dressing and living like the world. Though this church was a seemingly large church that was influential in their community, they had lost their fire for doing right.

However, in this church there were still a few Christians who had not lost their fire. There were still a few Christians who were still going after the souls of men. There were still a few Christians who had kept their standards. These were the Christians whom God commended in the verse above. I don't know, but I would imagine these few people were looked down upon by the rest of the church. I imagine that these few Christians were considered divisive by the rest of the church because of their stand. No doubt these few Christians were doing their best to keep the old-time religion alive in spite of the attacks of their fellow brethren. What's encouraging is that their effort to keep the old-time religion alive did not go unnoticed by God, and it kept God from destroying a church.

It has always been a few who have turned things around in a society or church. It was the three hundred men with whom Gideon fought that saved their nation. It was Jonathan and his armour bearer who fought and defeated the Philistines while the rest of the troops were sitting in fear of what they were going to do. It was one young boy by the name of David who stood against the giant of his day and saved his nation. It was the Prophet Elijah who stood alone against the wicked king that brought God's fire from Heaven. It was eleven disciples whom Jesus took and taught how to stand and reach a lost and dying world who influenced thousands to the point that they turned a world upside down for Christ.

Christian, you may feel that you are the only one who is standing against the world, but let me encourage you that it is always the few who turn the tide. You may think nobody notices your stand, and at times you can come to the point when you wonder, "What's the use?" Let me encourage you that God notices. Let me encourage you that it is your stand that gives one more chance for the old-time religion. You must not become weary in doing right, for God notices what you are doing. Your works and stand can certainly be the spark that turns things around.

Let me encourage you not to succumb to the pressures of compromise. When everyone else chides you for your vocal stand, you just keep on standing. Yes, there will be critics, but it is always the few who make a difference. All it takes is for the few to stop standing and to stop letting their voice be heard for evil and compromise to win. You may feel like a dinosaur in your generation for what you believe, but you keep standing by the old King James Bible. Just like God gave the church of Sardis a chance to see His blessings again, it could be your stand that causes your generation to see God's blessings again. When all seems to be hopeless, keep standing and don't despair!

The Lord God Reigneth

Revelation 19:6

"And I heard as it were the voice of a great multitude, and as the voice of many waters, and as the voice of mighty thunderings, saying, Alleluia: for the Lord God omnipotent reigneth."

There is coming a day when the LORD God will reign, not only in Heaven, but in all the Earth. God reminds us of this time in Revelation 19. We see in the verse above that right before God sets up His kingdom, the angels of Heaven get excited and begin to proclaim the greatness of God. This is certainly going to be a great day.

Though the millennial reign of Christ has not yet been set up on this Earth, I do believe that we can let Him reign in our hearts and lives. A Christian will never be totally satisfied with their life until Christ ruleth and reigneth as LORD. I find in Revelation what happens when Christ rules this Earth can be the same things that happen in your life if you will let Him reign as LORD.

First, when Christ reigns as LORD in your life, you will see His power revealed through you. Notice it says, *"the Lord God omnipotent reigneth."* Being omnipotent means having unlimited power. I believe one of the reasons Christians don't see the miracles of God in their life is because they don't allow Him to rule as LORD God. When God has total access of your life, you will begin to see the LORD unleash His power through you. When Christ is LORD of your life, you will see Him use His power through you to change lives, heal the broken hearted, lift the fallen, help the hurting and lead many to Jesus Christ for salvation. God's power will never be revealed through your life until you allow Him to reign in you.

Second, praise will come from your lips when Christ reigns as LORD in your life. When Christ is ruling your life, complaining and griping will not come from your lips. One of the reasons Christians gripe and complain is because they have never allowed Christ to rule their life. They're unhappy because they are allowing the world's system to rule their life which cannot bring praise. Praise will become common place for the Christian who allows Christ to reign in their life.

Third, verse 7 shows us that gladness fills the life of the Christian who allows Christ to reign in their life. You will never be pleased or delighted with your life until Christ reigns. Why are Christians unhappy with their lives? Because they have not let the Master make of their life what He wants it to be. Friend, God placed you on this Earth for a special task, and until you yield to Christ and let Him reign in your life, you will never be molded into the image of what Christ wants you to be.

Fourth, when Christ reigns in your life, you will rejoice over His goodness. One statement I often hear in churches is, "God is good, all the time." I love hearing this statement because it is true. When Christ rules in your life, you will see the goodness of God in everything you go through. You will never see the goodness of God through heartache and trials until Christ rules in your life.

Don't you desire these four things in your life? Only Christ ruling in your life will allow these things to be present. Stop yielding to the world and let Christ be the ruler of your life. I'm not talking about salvation, I'm talking about you taking your hands off the controls of your life and giving them to Christ. When He is ultimately the LORD God of your life is when you will see these four things all the time.

Achieving Satisfaction

Genesis 1:28

"And God blessed them, and God said unto them, Be fruitful, and multiply, and replenish the earth, and subdue it: and have dominion over the fish of the sea, and over the fowl of the air, and over every living thing that moveth upon the earth."

Satisfaction is not a destination, but it is a result of fulfilling your purpose in life. Far too many people seek for satisfaction through lifestyles and possessions and end up being dissatisfied with their life. There are people who have acquired houses, finances, automobiles and life's luxuries who are very dissatisfied.

The only way you will find satisfaction is to look at the purpose of why God placed you on this Earth. After God created Adam, He told him there were four things he was to do in life. God told him to *"Be fruitful, and multiply, and replenish the earth, and subdue it..."* In this little statement you find the formula to achieving satisfaction. Let me explain this formula to you.

First, God said to be fruitful. In other words, you are to be productive in life. Productivity takes hard work, but you will not find satisfaction without being productive. There are many people who end their day dissatisfied and that is because they were unproductive. You may recall some times in your life when at the end of the day you were worn out from a day of productivity, but you went to sleep that night totally satisfied because of your productivity. Idleness always produces dissatisfaction. Every day of your life there needs to be productivity to be satisfied with that day.

Second, God said to multiply. In other words, you need to grow in all that you do. I believe one of the reasons people struggle through the middle part of their life is because they have not grown. They are exactly where they were several years prior. You must constantly be growing in every area of your life. If you don't multiply what you do in life, you will never be satisfied.

Third, God said to replenish. The word *"replenish"* means to restore or fill up again. Satisfaction comes when you have replenished yourself in someone else. In other words, you will not be satisfied until you have helped someone to be able to do what you can do. I often say we need to train others to take our place when we are gone. None of us are guaranteed how long we have to live; therefore, you must constantly train others to take your place when you are gone. You will never be satisfied until you can look and see that your work will go on through others whom you have trained.

Finally, God said to subdue. Satisfaction comes from finishing projects. There is nothing like conquering something and then looking at it and realizing all the work it took to finish. One of the reasons an educational degree brings satisfaction is because you have conquered or subdued something. Every day of your life you need to finish something. You will never be satisfied with your day until you have finished something that day.

Friend, there is no great secret to satisfaction. You will never find it in possessions or lifestyles, but you will only find it in doing what God placed you on this Earth to do. Start filling each day with these four areas, and you will find yourself satisfied at the end of each day.

Responding to Tragedy

Job 1:20
"Then Job arose, and rent his mantle, and shaved his head, and fell down upon the ground, and worshipped,"

Maybe one of the reasons God thought so highly of Job is because of his response to tragedy. Before the tragedy hit Job, God knew how he would respond. It was not a guess on God's behalf of how Job would respond. When Satan came in from stalking God's people throughout the Earth, God asked him if he considered Job, a man *"that feared God, and eschewed evil."* Satan told God the only reason he was so good was because he had not faced tragedy. So, God gave him permission to touch his substance.

In one day Job lost about everything. I don't know the timeline, but the servants of Job were plowing in the field when the Sabeans came and took the oxen and servants away. When the one servant who escaped came to tell Job what happened, another servant came in and told him that fire fell from Heaven and consumed his sheep. That servant had barely finished talking when another servant came in to tell him that the Chaldeans stole all of his camels. That servant barely finished talking when another servant came and told him that all of his children were killed in a freak storm.

As a man, I can see Job's mind working as to how he would recover everything until he heard that his children were killed. We are not talking about one or two children dying in one day, but we are talking about ten children dying at the same time. There is no doubt that the hearts of he and his wife were devastated. They didn't get to give one last kiss. They didn't get to have one last hug. All they could do was go to the house where their children were and pull out their dead bodies. Oh the heartache that gripped the hearts of these parents.

Yet, how did Job respond when this tragedy struck his family? His first response was to fall on his face and worship God. Get this, he didn't fall on his face and gripe to God, but he fell on his face and gave reverence to God. As he worshipped God he said, *"Naked came I out of my mother's womb, and naked shall I return thither: the LORD gave, and the LORD hath taken away; blessed be the name of the LORD."* Wow, what a response! His response was to give homage to the One Who gave him life and thank Him for giving him the short amount of time he had with his children.

What is your response when tragedy strikes you? Job's response was not to look at what he had lost, but it was to look at what God had given him. This is what keeps a person from being depressed and suicidal. This is what keeps a person from going into their cocoon and hurting the rest of the relationships around them. When tragedy hits you must not look at what you have lost, instead you must look at what God gave you for the amount of time you had it.

Furthermore, the first person Job went to was God. His first response was to fall down and worship God. It was not to go to a spiritual friend and look for sympathy. His response was to go to the God Who is the source of all comfort and worship Him. That is the reason Job made it through such a tragic time.

Friend, if you will make your response to tragedy the same as Job's, then you will find that you can make it through any tragedy. Everyone is going to face some sort of tragedy in their life, and our first response should always be to fall down and worship God. Don't complain, but thank God for what He has given you and let His Holy Spirit comfort you through your tragedy. This is the only way to face tragedy and to keep tragedy from destroying you.

Age Isn't Everything

Job 15:10

"With us are both the grayheaded and very aged men, much elder than thy father."

I was very young when I started out in evangelism. I had barely made it through my twentieth year of life when I stepped out by faith into full-time evangelism. Because I was so young, one of the hardest things I had to overcome was the age barrier with those who were elderly, especially among the fraternity of preachers.

Now that I am in the middle years of life, I have the opportunity to help young men get started in the ministry. One of the common complaints I get from these young men is that they have a difficulty getting through the age barrier. It's as if the aged believe that a youth has nothing to teach them.

From my childhood I have learned to respect the aged. My parents always taught me to give up my seat to the aged. They taught me to address the aged properly by never addressing them by their first name. They also taught me to listen when in the presence of the aged so that I could learn from them. I'm thankful that they taught me these things for they have been very helpful to my advancement in life.

However, age doesn't always mean a person is wise or someone to whom I should listen. The friends of Job used their age and gray hairs as a defense of their attack against him. It was as if this was the golden grail of wisdom, and that he should listen to them because they were simply older than he. Yet, when I continue reading in the Book of Job, I find that it wasn't the aged person who had the right answers, but a younger man who respected the aged enough to let them speak first before he finally spoke on God's behalf.

Just because a person has age does not mean that you should follow their advice. There are many heathens who are aged. Does that mean that we should forget everything the Scriptures teach to follow their wicked advice? Certainly not! Just because a person has age does not mean they are a wise person. Just because a person has age does not mean they are worthy of being followed. Age is in no way a determining factor of whether someone's advice should be followed.

The determining factor on whether you should follow someone is whether they follow the Scriptures. The Scriptures are always the determining factor of right and wrong. Just because someone has inhabited this earth for many years does not mean they know more than God.

Furthermore, age doesn't always mean someone has common sense. One of the most disturbing things I find in our day is the lack of common sense. Common sense will help someone go a long way in life. Certainly someone with age should have more common sense because they have lived longer, but that isn't always the case.

This devotional is in no way a condemnation to the aged, but it is a caution in using age as the determining factor of whether you should listen to one's advice. Always remember the Scriptures are the final authority. If the aged don't follow the Scriptures, then the aged should not be followed. Yes, you should respect the aged and give them a hearing when they have walked in the pathway of the Scriptures, but don't think that age always makes them right.

Moreover, the aged person needs to give youth a break. I can certainly understand an aged person desiring the respect, but respect goes both ways. Don't belittle a person just because they are young. Give them a break and allow them the opportunity to do God's will for their life. Don't treat the youth as if they have no knowledge. Always remember that everyone is your teacher, this includes a youthful person who follows the Scriptures.

Turning Tragedy Into Triumph

Job 38:3

"Gird up now thy loins like a man; for I will demand of thee, and answer thou me."

You should never want tragedy to come your way and not get better through it. Your desire is that tragedy would make Job 23:10 come to life when it says, *"But he knoweth the way that I take: when he hath tried me, I shall come forth as gold."* There is no doubt that Job is the perfect picture of turning tragedy into triumph. I see there were five things that Job did that helped him to recover from tragedy and turn it into triumph.

First, if you are going to recover from tragedy you need to get up. One of the first words God said to Job when He addressed him was, *"Gird up now thy loins like a man..."* God was saying that Job had wallowed long enough in his self-pity and that it was time for him to get up and get going.

Wallowing in tragedy will not help you. I know when tragedy first hits the easiest thing to do is to go into hibernation and hope that you don't have to see anyone, but that will only make your hardship worse. When tragedy comes, you are purposely going to have to get up every day and live life. You are not the only one who has gone through tragedy, and you still have life to live. So, get up and live life.

Second, if you are going to recover from tragedy you need to look up. For the next several verses, God got Job to look up and see the great God Whom he served. Friend, there is only One Who can truly help you when tragedy comes, and you must look up to see Him. Looking to God is the only thing that will help you come out of tragedy the right way. He is the One Who can help you. When you get up, be sure to look up and see the God Who has the power to help you.

Third, if you are going to recover from tragedy you need to fess up. Job said in Job 40:4, *"Behold, I am vile; what shall I answer thee? I will lay mine hand upon my mouth."* Once Job looked up, he saw what he truly was, and he fessed up to God. Part of the reason God allows you to go through tragedy is so that you can get rid of sin so you can *"come forth as gold."* You will never fess up until you look up, and you will never look up until you get up. Once you look up and see where your weaknesses are, get them right so that God's refining process will work.

Fourth, if you are going to recover from tragedy you need to shut up. Look at Job 40:4 again, *"I will lay mine hand upon my mouth."* Friend, one of the things we must not do when tragedy comes is to whine and complain about it. You must realize that someone else always has it worse than you. When you whine and gripe about your tragedy, you are only showing others that you don't have a God Who is powerful enough to help you through it. Praise God instead of whining about your tragedy.

Fifth, if you are going to recover from tragedy you need to pray up. Job 42:10 says, *"And the LORD turned the captivity of Job, when he prayed for his friends:"* When going through tragedy you certainly want to pray to God about your heartache, but be sure to pray for others as well. It was when Job prayed for others that God turned the tragedy into triumph. Prayer is the only thing that turns tragedy into triumph. As long as you gripe and complain you cannot turn tragedy around. It will only happen when you pray, for prayer is the tool that engages the forces of Heaven to work on your behalf.

Turning tragedy into triumph starts when you get up. Whatever you face today can certainly be turned into triumph if you will get up and take the next four steps. Don't let tragedy destroy you, instead take tragedy and turn it into triumph by following these five steps. Let your tragedy become gold to which others can look to for encouragement through their tragedy.

Shirking Duties

Genesis 16:2

"And Sarai said unto Abram, Behold now, the LORD hath restrained me from bearing: I pray thee, go in unto my maid; it may be that I may obtain children by her. And Abram hearkened to the voice of Sarai."

One of the main causes of dysfunctional homes is that one or more family members are shirking their duties. When you look at Abram's home, you would have a hard time saying that it was not dysfunctional. He himself was the result of a dysfunctional home, and he didn't seem to overcome some of the problems that affected his upbringing. Then you look at Abram himself and see that there was lying, unfaithfulness and disrespect for each other. It is no wonder that his home was dysfunctional. Yet, there were two main things that led to the dysfunction in his home.

First, Sarai shirked her duty of following and pressured Abram to let her take the reins of household leadership. From the beginning God never intended for the wife to take the leadership role. Because Abram and Sarai had no children, and because their desire for a child was great, Sarai pressured her husband into going in unto their maid to try and have a child through her. Sarai stepped out of her role of following her husband and her influence over her husband led in part to the dysfunction in their home.

Ladies, the power you have over your husband is great. You can use that power to get your way, but that will only lead to a dysfunctional home. Your silence when your husband decides to do something you don't want to do is your way of manipulating your husband into doing what you want to do. There are also some ladies who are not manipulative about not following their husband, but they just won't follow and they make that known. You may get what you want, but your unwillingness to follow your husband's leadership will lead to a dysfunctional home. Ladies, you must be careful that you don't use your influence to pressure your husband into doing something that will lead to a dysfunctional home.

Second, Abram shirked his duty of leadership. It doesn't matter how much pressure Sarai put on her husband, he should have never allowed her pressure to cause him to step down from the role of leader in the home. When he shirked his duty as the leader in the home, it led to dysfunction that continued to follow his family.

Men, your job is to be the leader in your home. When you shirk your duty of leadership, you cause your home to become dysfunctional. I don't care how much pressure your wife may put on you, and it really doesn't matter how uncomfortable the pressure may be. You are a man, and you should lead no matter what pressure is applied. Far too many men shirk their duty of leadership in the home because they just don't want to put up with the grief their wife will give. Men, if you want your home to be what it ought to, then you need to lead your home.

Every dysfunctional home can be traced back to either the husband or wife shirking their duties. The duty of the wife is to follow her husband's leadership, and the duty of the husband is to lead the home. If both husband and wife will fulfill their duty in the home, then you will find a home that operates properly and a home that is filled with peace.

Selfish Parenting

Genesis 25:28

"And Isaac loved Esau, because he did eat of his venison: but Rebekah loved Jacob."

You would think that Isaac would have learned from his parents the dangers of selfish parenting. He saw firsthand what happens if parents become selfish, because he dealt with it through his step brother, Ishmael. Yet, we find that Isaac and Rebekah both got involved in selfish parenting which led to sibling rivalry in the home. The sibling rivalry didn't stop in the home. It followed them throughout their young adult lives. There were three very selfish things Jacob and Rebekah did that led to the sibling rivalry of Jacob and Esau.

First, they played favorites with their boys. It says that Jacob loved Esau but Rebekah loved Jacob. This no doubt affected the way they treated their sons. It probably affected the way they punished their children as well as their time spent with each child.

Parents have to be very careful that they don't play favorites with their children. Every child must be loved the same. Yes, you may love each child in their unique way, but you cannot give any perception of favorites. This creates a rivalry atmosphere among children. Children need the security that they are as loved from both parents as each of their siblings. God certainly does this with His children. God doesn't love one child more than another just because one is better than the other. Just because one child may act a little better, you must never portray that you love them more than the child who may be a little more challenging to raise.

Second, they manipulated circumstances in the home by using their children. When Rebekah saw that Esau was going to be blessed, she used Jacob as a tool of manipulation to be sure he was blessed and not Esau. Using your children to manipulate your spouse to get what you want only teaches your children to manipulate things to get what they want. Children don't need to be taught to use manipulation to get what they want, because manipulation is dishonesty. You may use your children to manipulate circumstances, but eventually you will find they will begin to manipulate you to get what they want. Instead of teaching your children how to manipulate situations to get what they want, you should teach them to be honest and work hard to get what they want.

Third, they wanted to be friends to their children instead of parents. Both Isaac and Rebekah were guilty of trying to be their favorite child's friend instead of being a parent and correcting them when they did wrong. This selfish style of parenting only causes you to lose your children in the end. You are not supposed to be your child's friend, you are supposed to be their parent. Sometimes a parent must make tough decisions that will cause their child not to like them, but that is being a parent. Parents must rear their children to do right, and many times that will cause them to dislike your decisions.

Friend, parenting is not an easy task, but selfish parenting only makes parenting harder. Be careful that you don't become selfish in your parenting. Selfish parenting leads to selfish children, and having selfish children leads to sibling rivalry. If you don't want your home to be a battleground of sibling rivalry, don't be guilty of being a selfish parent.

Surrounded by Deceit

Genesis 40:23

"Yet did not the chief butler remember Joseph, but forgat him."

Have you ever felt that your life is constantly on the bad end of lies? What I mean by this statement is that you are the one who is lied about and is considered the bad guy. This is certainly a helpless feeling, and can also drive a person to try to get revenge.

Nobody epitomizes this better than Joseph. Joseph's early life seems to be one that was surrounded by deceit. His father was a master of deceit, and it is very obvious that Joseph's brothers learned it from him. Then, Joseph's brothers practiced their deceit on him and sold him into slavery. When Joseph must have thought it couldn't get any worse, it did. His master's wife lied about him trying to force himself upon her which resulted in his imprisonment. Finally, while in prison the inmates whom he helped promised to speak a good word to Pharaoh, and they did not. Somehow, through about thirty years of deceit that surrounded Joseph, he came through life with a good attitude and did not let the deceit destroy him.

There are going to be times in your life when you are going to be the recipient of deceit. When that happens, what you do with it will determine what your attitude is and what God can do with you. There were four definite things Joseph did that helped him deal with deceit in a good way.

First, Joseph kept doing right. It would have been easy to give up and say, "What's the use?", but he didn't do that. He kept on doing right because he was not going to allow the bad character of others to affect his. When you are the recipient of deceit, you must keep doing right. Don't lower yourself to the character level of those who are deceitful. Remember, God is watching and will reward both you and the deceitful ones. Don't reward deceit with deceit, instead keep doing right.

Second, Joseph kept helping people. This is truly amazing when you consider how many people were deceitful towards him. You cannot adopt the attitude that everyone is deceitful so you are not going to help anyone. When you are the recipient of deceit, don't allow it to cause you to lose your belief in the goodness of people. Keep helping people, for there are plenty of good people whom you can help, and your action to help is what will get you through the damages of deceit.

Third, Joseph saw the whole picture. This is the part that truly amazes me about Joseph. He understood there was a bigger picture than the immediate, and that is what kept him going. When you are the recipient of deceit, don't forget to look at the bigger picture. You are only living in a small time frame of your life, and you must pull yourself back to see the whole picture and realize that God is in control. You must realize that God is using this deceit for some good. You may not be able to see the good, but it will come if you look at the whole picture and realize that God is in control.

Finally, Joseph didn't give up. He kept going and believed that this part of his life would end, and it did. Whatever you do, you must keep going when you are the recipient of deceit. There are many people who are still depending upon you to keep going. Joseph didn't understand how many people were truly depending upon him, but there were thousands of people who would have died had he given up. You don't know what your future may be and that is why you must not give up. God is going to use you if you will keep a good attitude through the deceit and continue to do what is right. Don't let the helpless feeling that deceit has dropped upon you cause you to quit. Just keep on going realizing that it is all part of a bigger picture of God's plan to use you.

Don't Go Too Far

Exodus 8:28

"And Pharaoh said, I will let you go, that ye may sacrifice to the LORD your God in the wilderness; only ye shall not go very far away: intreat for me."

Moses nearly made the same mistake that many pastors and Christians make had not God stepped in and stopped it. As Moses continued to challenge Pharaoh's attempt to let them go and sacrifice to God, Pharaoh came back and offered Moses to sacrifice to God, but he said *"ye shall not go very far away."* Moses actually agreed to the offer, but God stepped in and hardened Pharaoh's heart so that he would not let them go.

I'm sure this offer didn't sound too bad to Moses. You must understand the pressure Moses had coming from both Pharaoh and his own people. Moses probably thought that this compromise was a way to relieve the pressure. What Moses didn't understand is that if he had gone through with this offer, Pharaoh would have known that they were not very serious because they moved one time.

This same offer to not go very far away is what you are faced with on a day-to-day basis. Satan initially attacks the Christian with unreasonable offers that he knows they will not accept, and then he comes back with the offer to not go very far away. Satan knows that if you don't go too far from the world that he will eventually get you to come back to the world. He knows that as long as the world is in sight that its allure and fancies will eventually cause you to come back. The offer to not go too far away must never be accepted.

We must be careful about our churches accepting the offer to stay close to the world. Many pastors have gotten tired of not seeing their churches grow, and they think that if they don't go too far from the world that it will bring the world into the church. This is not the case! Pastors must realize that if the world can get the church to move, they will continue to apply pressure for the church to get closer until they are no longer serving the LORD. The pastor must never accept the world's offer of not going too far away. The church must stand with truth, for truth will take the world's viewpoint completely out of sight.

Moreover, every home must be careful about not accepting the offer of staying closer to the world. Parents, don't become weary of the constant barrage of attacks from your teenager to let up. The Devil would love for you to move your home where it is not too far from the world. Many homes have been destroyed because they stayed in eyeshot of the world only to completely stop serving the LORD to the detriment of their children.

Furthermore, every Christian needs to be careful about allowing the enticement of not going too far away. You may become weary with the criticism about your stand from work or school, but you must never allow the world's offer to come closer to cause you to move. Friend, they are waiting for you to move one time. If you move once then you have lost the battle. You must continue to stand strong and not move even if the world calls you extreme.

Always remember that when God saved you, He brought you out of the world. The whole reason the world wants you to not go too far is so that you can still see the temptations of the world. The answer is to stay close to God. You are a Christian, and you should never leave God's side. If you will stay close to God, the call of not going too far will never entice you.

Remember the Bones

Exodus 13:19

"And Moses took the bones of Joseph with him: for he had straitly sworn the children of Israel, saying, God will surely visit you; and ye shall carry up my bones away hence with you."

The last words of Joseph were, *"And Moses took the bones of Joseph with him: for he had straitly sworn the children of Israel, saying, God will surely visit you; and ye shall carry up my bones away hence with you."* (Genesis 50:25) Those bones that Moses took with him as he exited Egypt were more than a set of bones; they represented something much greater. The meaning of those bones were so great that Moses carried the bones. He didn't have Aaron or one of the Levites take them, he took them because he was the leader. He understood the importance of what those bones meant to Israel, and he wanted to be sure that the meaning of those bones were not forgotten.

First, those bones represented that God fulfills His promises. The last words Joseph said was that God would *"visit"* Israel and bring them back to the Promised Land. Moses wanted the people to be reminded that God always fulfills his promise.

Every Christian needs to be sure that they keep God's fulfilled promises in sight. It is interesting that it took four hundred years before the promise was fulfilled, but God always keeps His promise. You must always remember to look at the fulfilled promises of God so that you don't give up when God has not yet fulfilled a promise in your life. God will fulfill His promises in his timing, and sometimes His timing is much longer than we would want. Always remember that the bones are God's promises fulfilled.

Second, those bones represented their heritage. Though Egypt forgot their heritage, Moses didn't want Israel to forget theirs. He understood that if Israel was going to keep God's blessings on their lives, then they must never forget their heritage. Likewise, you must remember the bones of your heritage. Don't look at your heritage as a bunch of dead bones, but look at those bones and remember who you are and from whence you came.

Third, carrying those bones out of Egypt was a sign to the rest of the people that Moses was going to carry on what his forefathers passed down to him. Friend, every generation needs to pick up the bones of their heritage and carry it on. All it takes is for one generation to decide not to carry the bones, and the next generation will forget their heritage. Your children and grandchildren will only learn God's heritage if you carry the bones. Don't be negligent because it inconveniences you or is unpopular. Carry those bones for that is the only way the next generation will understand their heritage.

Fourth, those bones represented the responsibility of everyone carrying them. Moses wanted to be the one to carry the bones so that everyone from the top down would understand the importance. Keeping your heritage alive is everyone's responsibility. We cannot just leave it to a few to fight to keep it alive, but every person must understand it is their responsibility to carry the bones of their heritage.

Are you carrying the bones of your heritage or have you laid them aside because they seem antiquated? Christian, we live in times when people are forsaking the bones of their heritage for something new, and it takes people like you to carry the bones. Don't be ashamed of carrying the bones of your heritage. Carry them proudly and openly so that there is no mistake that you represent the God of Heaven and that you are not ashamed of what He has made of you.

Salvaging a People

Exodus 29:14

"But the flesh of the bullock, and his skin, and his dung, shalt thou burn with fire without the camp: it is a sin offering."

I seriously doubt that we will ever understand the sacrifice Christ made to save us from our sins. When you look at the sacrifices God commanded the children of Israel to observe, you get a small picture of the sacrifice Christ made for mankind. The sacrifice that He made shows the great love that He has for every person.

In the verse above, God commanded Moses to offer a sin offering for Aaron and his sons as a part of setting them apart for the office of the priest. God told them to take a bullock and kill it at the door of the tabernacle. Then they were to take the blood of the bullock and spear it on the horns of the altar and pour the remaining blood at the bottom of the altar. They were then to flay the bullock and sacrifice the inwards of it, but they were to take the skin and the dung and burn them with fire without the camp. In this sacrifice is a picture of what Jesus did to salvage mankind, but I also believe it takes the same from you to be an influence on people to help bring them to Christ. Let me take this sacrifice and show you what it will take for you to be used to salvage people.

First, you must be willing to be a sacrifice. One of the most interesting things about Christ being our sacrifice is that He had to be willing to leave Heaven for you and I. If you are not willing to sacrifice yourself for others, you will never have the influence upon them to change their lives. Jesus left everything so that He could save a world from their sins, and until you are willing to leave everything for others, you will never have the impact on their lives to see them changed.

Second, you must love them enough to go where they are. Jesus didn't stay in Heaven to salvage mankind, but He left a wonderful place to go to a horrible place all because He loved man so much that He wanted them to be saved from their sins. You will never greatly influence people until they see you love them more than anything else. Until you are willing to go where they are, you will never make a change in their life. I'm not talking about living their lifestyle, but I'm talking about being among them and not being ashamed to bring them to Christ. If you only want to stay in the comforts of your church and home, you will not reach them. You must go to where people are if you are going to salvage them.

Third, you must lay aside the robes of who you are if you are going to salvage a people. One of the most interesting things about this sacrifice is that the bullock had its skin removed. This was symbolic of Jesus laying aside His robes of Deity and taking on the robes of humanity so that we could be reached. Don't get me wrong, Jesus Christ was still God, but He took on flesh so that He could reach us. You will never reach people and salvage them if you are not willing to change who you are to become like Christ. You can become stubborn and say that you are not going to change, but you will never reach people. You must realize that God cannot change people through you until you lay aside your robes of humanity to be clothed with the power of the Holy Spirit of God. It is when we take on His likeness that we can influence others.

I ask you, are you willing to do what it takes to salvage people? Jesus Christ was willing to do all of this to salvage you, the least you can do is follow His example to try to salvage those in your world. People are needing you. Be that person who is willing to take these steps to salvage a people for the sake of Christ.

Preparing for God

Leviticus 9:4

"Also a bullock and a ram for peace offerings, to sacrifice before the LORD; and a meat offering mingled with oil: for to day the LORD will appear unto you."

I fear too often we are very flippant about how we come to God in prayer. Because Jesus died on the cross, we have clear access to God through prayer at any time. This access to God can be taken for granted if we are not careful, which will cause us to come before God unprepared.

The children of Israel were not flippant at all when it came to God's presence. In the verse above, God told Israel that He would *"appear unto you."* You can only imagine the excitement, and yet the fear they had in their hearts to have God appear to them. This was not a common occurrence. To prepare for God's presence, they were told several things they were to do, and those same things we also should do as we prepare to go into His presence.

First, confess your sin. In verse 2, they were told to take a calf and offer a sin offering. They were going into the presence of a holy God, and in His presence there must be no sin. Before you ever enter the closet of prayer, I believe it is wise to take the time to confess your sin to God. You must not go into His presence with the filth of the world upon you. Ask the Holy Spirit to show you the sins in your life, and as He reveals them to you confess them to God so that you may be clean when you enter His presence.

Second, have a place where you meet God. Verse 5 talks about the children of Israel coming close to the tabernacle to meet with God. I believe it would be a good thing that you have a place where you meet with God on a regular basis. Make it a place that is more sacred than others. Certainly, we can go to God at any time and in any place, but that place where you go to daily meet with Him should be a place that is set apart in your mind for Him.

Third, have a set time to meet with God. Again in verse 5, they came together at a certain time to meet with God. Let me again encourage you to have a set time when you regularly meet with God. I believe the best time to do this is earlier in the day, and preferably before you set out to do business. You are going into the presence of God, and I believe there should be a respect of Who He is, and setting a time will help you to do that.

Third, take the time to thank God for the blessings in your life. Throughout this chapter you see God talked often about burning the fat upon the altar. This is symbolic of the blessings of God. There are so many blessings that come our way that we should not have any problems with thanking God for them. This is all to help remind you of your helplessness without an Almighty God.

Finally, don't take coming into God's presence for granted. Right after God met with the children of Israel, you see Nadab and Abihu offering strange fire upon the altar. God killed them for this strange fire, for God wanted the fire to ever be burning. I believe what they did was they took for granted that they were in God's presence, and that is why it didn't bother them to offer the strange fire.

Though God may not kill you for being flippant in His presence, you should not tempt Him to do so. Always be reverential as you come into His presence. Go into His presence understanding the privilege you have to do this. I believe when you do this you will find your time with God is more sacred and fulfilling. Be sure the next time you pray that you take the time to prepare yourself for God, and you will find a more satisfying prayer life.

All These Rules

Leviticus 11:2

"Speak unto the children of Israel, saying, These are the beasts which ye shall eat among all the beasts that are on the earth."

Most of todays Christianity would not survive in the Old Testament times because of all the rules God had for His people. God had rules on what they could and could not eat. He had rules on how they were to dress. He had rules on who they could marry. He had rules on how they were to interact with each other. These rules that God had were not loose by any stretch of the imagination, but they were very strict rules by which they were to live. If they lived by these rules, the blessings God promised were tremendous; but, if they disobeyed them the punishments were severe. As I look at these rules, I learn that there are several things these rules reveal about God's people today.

First, rules reveal the heart of God's people. The rules showed whether the people were tenderhearted and wanted to do right, or if their hearts were filled with bitterness and rebellion. The same is true today. God's rules are restrictive, but they are restricting you from heartache. Those who fight against God's rules are only revealing their heart. So many preachers today say that you will run people off with the rules of Christianity, and they try to loosen God's expectations of His children. God has these rules and expects us to live by them so that they can reveal our heart to Him and to our leaders. The restrictiveness of rules is not restrictive to the obedient and tenderhearted, they are only restrictive to the disobedient and rebellious.

Second, rules reveal your love for God. John 14:15 says, *"If ye love me, keep my commandments."* When a person fights against God's rules, they are only revealing their lack of love and respect for Him. For instance, I love my wife and she loves me. We both have rules for each other, and out of love and respect we keep those rules. Likewise the Christian who keeps God's rules is the Christian who loves God the most.

Third, rules reveal your direction to the world. One of the reasons God set these rules up for Israel was to show to the rest of the world that they were different. God didn't want Israel to look like and live like the rest of the world. They were God's people. Likewise, the reason God has rules for His children is because He wants the world to see that you are not going its direction, but your direction in life is to live for God. Sadly, many Christians today look more like the world than they do a Christian. Their lack of obedience to God's Word is simply showing that their direction is worldly. Those who obey God's rules are showing they want to be different from the world.

Fourth, rules reveal your desires. Verse 45 says, "For I am the LORD that bringeth you up out of the land of Egypt, to be your God: ye shall therefore be holy, for I am holy." God set up these rules to make Israel holy as He is holy. Friend, when you live by God's rules, you are showing that you have a heart that desires holiness. The more you obey God's rules, the more like Him you become which results in holiness. Rules simply reveal whether or not your true desire is to be holy.

How do you feel about the rules of God? Do you fight against them and try to lower them? God's rules do have a purpose, and that purpose is to reveal your heart, love, direction and desires for God. I encourage you not to view God's rules as restrictive, rather let them give you the freedom to be more like Him.

The Rest Principle

Leviticus 25:4

"But in the seventh year shall be a sabbath of rest unto the land, a sabbath for the LORD: thou shalt neither sow thy field, nor prune thy vineyard."

This devotional is not for the lazy person. This devotional is for the person who finds themselves guilty because they are not working. There are many people who can feel guilty when they stop to rest, but they must understand that God gives us a rest principle on purpose.

In the verse above, God gives the rest principle when it came to planting crops. He said that every seventh year they were to let their land rest so that it could be more productive. You find that God instituted the rest principle at the very beginning. For six days God worked, but on the seventh day He rested. You will notice that every seventh day or year there is a needed rest. That is what we would call the rest principle.

It is important for your health and productivity to practice the rest principle in your life. You cannot go nonstop without any rest without something breaking down. Either your health, relationships, spiritual well-being or productivity will break down if you don't learn to have a time to rest on a regular basis. Let me share with you several thoughts concerning the rest principle.

First, there is nothing about which to feel guilty when you rest. I'm a person that many would call a workaholic. I find myself constantly working, and even at times will feel guilty when I take time off. I have had to learn to remind myself that God took time to rest. If you are a hard worker, you must not feel guilty about taking time to rest because it is a command of God to have a regular time to rest.

Second, rest only comes after work. In each instance when God commands us to rest, it is always done after work. God worked six days and then He rested. The land is worked for six years and then it is to be rested. You don't rest and then work, but you work and then rest. The rest principle is only for those who have obeyed God and worked.

Third, rest must be planned. This is so important for those who find it hard within themselves to take time to rest. If you don't plan a day that you take off, then you won't do it. If you don't plan a time to take vacation, then you won't ever take a vacation. Plan time off in your schedule and obey your scheduled time off.

Fourth, rest must be regular. You will notice that God planned the seventh day to be a day of rest each week. God was establishing the importance of taking a regular time off away from work. Just as it is important to take time off to rest, it is also as important to make it regular. God made your body with a need to rest.

Friend, rest is an important part of your life if you are going to be productive in every area. Church leaders must be careful that they give their people time to rest if they want their church to be productive. Employers must be sure that they require their employees to take time off to rest. Individuals need to have a regular time off to rest. Without rest you are setting yourself up to break down physically, mentally and spiritually. Many people have fallen into sin because they were too tired to fight temptation. Many people have become sickly because they haven't rested. If the rest principle is followed in your life, you will find that you will have more energy to do what God wants you to do, and that your productivity will increase.

What Do You See?

Numbers 13:17-18

"And Moses sent them to spy out the land of Canaan, and said unto them, Get you up this way southward, and go up into the mountain: And see the land, what it is; and the people that dwelleth therein, whether they be strong or weak, few or many;"

God told Moses to choose twelve men, one from each tribe, to go into the land of Canaan to spy out the land and to come back and tell the people what they saw. For forty days these men were in the land of Canaan and saw the future that God had promised to them. Sadly, when they came back, ten men gave an evil report and two men gave a positive report. Because of the evil report of the ten men, the children of Israel followed the advice of the ten men to their detriment.

It is interesting that these twelve spies saw the same thing, but they really didn't see the same thing. They all saw the iron chariots. They all saw the huge walls of defense. They all saw the giants of the land. They all saw the grapes of Eschol and the blessing in the land. Yet, they all saw these things through a different perspective. Ten men saw these things through fleshly eyes, while two men saw these things through the eyes of faith. The ten men who saw these things through fleshly eyes had the evil report, while the two men who saw these things through the eyes of faith had the same perspective as God.

Let me give you a friendly warning not to look at things through fleshly eyes. When you look at things through fleshly eyes you will not see the potential of God's power. Joshua and Caleb saw what God could do in the land of Canaan. They said, *"Let us go up at once, and possess it; for we are well able to overcome it."* When you see things through the eyes of faith you will always see things in a positive light of what God can do; however, if you see things through eyes of flesh you will always see the obstacles.

Christian, be careful to look at your church and the works of God through the eyes of faith. Don't be negative about everything going on in your church. Certainly, there may be things that need to be corrected, but don't complain and gripe about everything you see in the church. It could be that the reason you see the negative is because you are looking through fleshly eyes. It could be that your eyes of faith are weak and need to be strengthened through the Word of God. You will find that when you look through the eyes of faith, God will change your perspective to see things His way.

I encourage you to daily ask God to help you see things through the eyes of faith. When you find yourself being negative, stop what you are doing and get alone and ask God to help you see things through His eyes. Don't always assume that you are seeing things correctly. Let the eyes of faith cause you to see the power of God working through the obstacles that the eyes of faith see. Let the eyes of faith cause you to see opportunities and not barriers.

Your perception will ultimately determine what God will do through you. Ten men who could have seen the power of God knock down the walls, crush the iron chariots and defeat the giants never saw it because of the negative their eyes of flesh caused them to see. Is your perception keeping you from seeing the miraculous? Yield your eyes to God and let Him control them to see through the eyes of faith. It is then that you will begin to see what the power of God can do to remove every obstacle that stands in your way.

Another

Numbers 23:27

"And Balak said unto Balaam, Come, I pray thee, I will bring thee unto another place; peradventure it will please God that thou mayest curse me them from thence."

Balaam missed one of the greatest opportunities of his lifetime because he continually listened to another offer from Balak to curse the children of Israel. If Balaam had stood his ground, he may have been able to turn Balak to right. Instead, Balak initially came to Balaam and asked him to come and curse Israel, but because God told him not to go, he sent the servant of Balak away. When they came back with another offer, Balaam accepted it and went, but God interceded and kept Balaam from doing something that he would regret more than he already did. The four offers Balak offered Balaam to justify the sin is the interesting part of this story.

The first offer was to go to another place. It says in the verse above, *"I pray thee, I will bring thee unto another place..."* Balak thought that going to another place would not make something wrong. If something is wrong in one place, it is wrong in all places. One of the amazing things that I watch Christians do is avoid something in one place because they say it would be bad, but they will do it in another place. Sin is sin no matter where you do it. Going to another place doesn't make something right. If it would be wrong to smoke a cigarette in the church auditorium, it would be wrong to smoke anywhere. If it is wrong to curse in front of the preacher, it is wrong to curse anywhere. You must be careful that you don't fall for the trap of justifying sin because it is in another place.

The second offer was to give him another position. Balak said in Numbers 24:11, *"I thought to promote thee unto great honour..."* Just because Balaam would have a higher position doesn't make sin right. Another problem I often see in Christianity is that we fall for the lie that our position justifies the sin. Again, it does not matter what your position may be, it is never right to commit sin. If it is wrong for the church member to do something, it is wrong for the pastor to do it. If it is wrong for a child to do something, it is wrong for the parent to do it. Your position never justifies wrong.

The third offer was to give him another wealth. Balaam said in Numbers 24:13, *"If Balak would give me his house full of silver and gold, I cannot go beyond the commandment of the Lord…"* Balak thought that he could buy his way out of sin, but money cannot buy you out of sin. Friend, God doesn't care how much money you have, your checking account balance never justifies sin. Just because you may buy your way out of trouble with man does not mean you can buy your way out of trouble with God. Money never justifies a wrong.

The fourth offer was to give him another fame. Balak said that he wanted to give Balaam *"great honour."* In other words, he was going to make him famous. Just because you can have more influence does not justify compromise or sin. If you must compromise or sin to attain more influence, the influence itself is wrong. You can justify your compromise by saying that if you have more influence you can lead more people to Christ, but that doesn't justify sin.

Christian, do you find yourself justifying your sin because of one of the other offers? Always keep in mind that sin is sin no matter how you put it. Always do right! Don't let the offers of this world's Balak's cause you to sin. Always do right and let God be the one who promotes you unto honor.

It's Time to Move On

Deuteronomy 1:6

"The LORD our God spake unto us in Horeb, saying, Ye have dwelt long enough in this mount:"

Horeb is a two-mile long mountain range that had significant impact upon the children of Israel. In this mountain range is Mount Sinai; the mount where Moses received the ten commandments. This is the mountain range where the rock of Horeb was; the rock from which the water came out. As you can see, Horeb had a significant spiritual impact on God's people.

However, God told Israel, *"Ye have dwelt long enough in this mount:"* God was telling them they needed to move on. I'm sure it would have been great to dwell beside the mount where God met with Moses, but it was time to move on. Certainly it would have been a wonderful time to see the water continually flow from the rock of Horeb, but they needed to move on. If they dwelt by Horeb, then they would have never conquered the Promised Land. If they dwelt by Horeb, they would have never seen the great victory of Jericho. Yes, they needed Horeb, but after Horeb they needed to move on so God could show His power through them.

It is highly important that every Christian understand the value of Horeb and moving on. You need to spend time daily at Horeb and study the Scriptures. You need that time at the rock of Horeb where you drink of the waters of God; however, you can't live there and see God do great things through you. You need to move on and take what you learned in Horeb so that you can see the victories throughout the day in your Promised Land. There are several reasons you need to move on from Horeb.

First, you will never grow proportionately if you don't move on from Horeb. Certainly, you need to spend time with God in the Scriptures, but the purpose of you learning the Scriptures is so that you can serve Him throughout the day. There are many Christians who are spiritually fat from the Scriptures, but they never take what they have learned to serve God. The reason God teaches you the Scriptures is so that you can use those truths to serve Him. You will never properly grow spiritually if you don't move on and take what you have learned from Horeb.

Second, you will never have great miracles in your life if you don't move on from Horeb. There were significant miracles that Israel experienced after they left Horeb. If they had stayed at Horeb, those miracles would have never been experienced. You will never see great victories in your life without taking what you learned in Horeb to serve God. God has victories and miracles planned for you, but you must move on and serve God throughout the day.

Third, you will never live in your Promised Land if you don't move on from Horeb. The Promised Land was God's will for Israel. God has a will for your life that you will never experience if you don't move on. God's will is not simply a place, but it is an action. It is the act of obeying what you learned in Horeb.

Christian, you cannot have the miracles and victories in your life without moving on from Horeb. You need to daily go to your Mount Sinai and rock of Horeb to spend time with God, but then you need to move on from what you have learned throughout the week and help those whom God leads across your paths. Don't avoid your Horeb, but don't stay at your Horeb, move on. Both are needed if you are going to live a victorious Christian life.

Don't Avoid Mercy and Grace

Psalm 116:4-5

"Then called I upon the name of the LORD; O LORD, I beseech thee, deliver my soul. Gracious is the LORD, and righteous; yea, our God is merciful."

Most of the trouble in which we find ourselves is our own fault. Certainly there are times when trouble comes our way that we have done nothing to cause, but the majority of the time our troubles are self-inflicted. When this happens, we tend to avoid running to God to ask for His help. The Devil whispers in our ear that we don't deserve God's help and that we shouldn't bother Him with something that we caused. Though the Devil may be right in that we don't deserve God's help, that still shouldn't keep us from going to God to ask Him for help.

The psalmist said in verse 3, *"I found trouble and sorrow."* Notice, trouble and sorrow didn't find the psalmist, but he found it. In other words, he is the one who caused his own trouble and sorrow. Yet, though he caused his own trouble and sorrow, he didn't avoid the mercy and grace of God. He understood that God would be merciful and gracious if he would simply call upon Him. There are several things we learn about God in this psalm that will be helpful to us.

First, God's ear is never deafened to His children. Verse 1 says, *"I love the LORD, because he hath heard my voice and my supplications."* God heard his voice when he found *"trouble and sorrow."* We often think that God only hears us when we are good, but you must remember that God also hears you when you are bad. God is One Who will help us out of our troubles even when we are the ones who caused them.

Second, God has the tendency to listen intently for His children. Verse 2 says, *"Because he hath inclined his ear unto me..."* The word *"inclined"* means, having a tendency. God knows we are going to get ourselves in trouble, so He purposely is listening for our call. Do you understand what this means? God is anxious to help you out of your troubles even if you caused them. This should excite you. It should humble you that God is very gracious to help us, and wants to help us in all our troubles.

Third, God is willing to deliver us out of the troubles that our sin caused. Verse 3 says, *"The sorrows of death compassed me..."* Remember, according to Romans 6:23, sin causes death. God is saying that even though our sin has caused our troubles, He is still willing to deliver us from them. What an amazing God to deliver us when our own actions of sin have caused our troubles. Just because you have sinned does not mean God doesn't want to help you. God wants to help you in your troubles even when your sins have caused them.

Friend, God is simply showing that His mercy and grace is available to you if you will call unto Him in your troubles. I don't know what your troubles are, but don't avoid the One Who can help you with them. If your sin caused your trouble, then you most certainly cannot get yourself out of the trouble. You need God to help you out of them. Don't let the Devil steal God's help from you. Don't let your pride keep you from getting God's help. No matter what the trouble is that you face today, call upon the LORD and ask for His deliverance. His grace and mercy is available if you will simply ask.

Wasting God's Power

Joshua 2:10

"For we have heard how the LORD dried up the water of the Red sea for you, when ye came out of Egypt; and what ye did unto the two kings of the Amorites, that were on the other side Jordan, Sihon and Og, whom ye utterly destroyed."

The children of Israel were at the brink of the Jordan River. Forty years had passed since they were at this point, and now they were ready to go and take the Promised Land.

Just like before, Joshua sent men to spy out the land. As the men toured the land, they saw the bounty that God had for them. Word came to the leaders of the land that there were spies spying out the land, so these men had to hide in the house of Rahab the harlot before they could go back and give their report.

While in the Rahab's house she said to them, *"I know that the LORD hath given you the land, and that your terror is fallen upon us, and that all the inhabitants of the land faint because of you."* This was certainly an encouraging report to hear. She wanted her family saved from the impending invasion, and she told these men that the inhabitants of the land were fearful of them.

Moreover, she continued in the verse above and said, *"For we have heard how the LORD dried up the water of the Red sea for you, when ye came out of Egypt; and what ye did unto the two kings of the Amorites, that were on the other side Jordan, Sihon and Og, whom ye utterly destroyed."* Hold on! Now she was talking about forty years prior to these spies being in her house. She told them that the land was fearful **since the time** that God parted the Red Sea.

What this lady said is much different than what the ten spies said to Moses. They said in Numbers 13:28-29, *"Nevertheless the people be strong that dwell in the land, and the cities are walled, and very great: and moreover we saw the children of Anak there.*

The Amalekites dwell in the land of the south: and the Hittites, and the Jebusites, and the Amorites, dwell in the mountains: and the Canaanites dwell by the sea, and by the coast of Jordan." What Rahab painted was a much different picture than what these men depicted. This means for forty years God's power had been wasted. What could have been forty years of God's power being revealed was wasted because of a lack of faith on the behalf of these ten spies.

I'm afraid that we often waste God's power in our lives because of our lack of faith. These ten spies should have trusted God's Word like Joshua and Caleb did, and they would have seen the power of God help them to conquer the land. Likewise, our lack of faith in God always wastes God's power being performed in our lives.

The only thing standing between you and God's power working through your life is whether you choose to trust God and step out by faith or to trust your flesh. Christian, God wants to work through your life, but you must obey what He tells you to do. When you forsake the paths that God commands you to walk in to try new paths that seem to be more workable for this day, then you are wasting what God will do through you if you will obey. Always remember what God tells you to do may not seem to be feasible, but He has already done the work for your faith just like He did for Israel forty years prior to them coming in.

Don't waste God's power in your life. Obey Him and what He commands you to do and you will not have to waste years of your life wandering in faithlessness; instead, you can spend those years experiencing the power of God working through you.

Blinding Affects

Joshua 8:15

"And Joshua and all Israel made as if they were beaten before them, and fled by the way of the wilderness."

"How could I not see it?" This is one of the most common questions a person asks themselves after sin has conquered them. Sin has a way of blinding us from its affect on our lives, and we often don't see these affects until it's too late and we have already experienced its destructing hands.

Israel is a perfect picture of how sin blinds us from its affects. During the battle of Jericho, Achan sinned by taking of the accursed things. Though Achan hid his sin well, its affect caused Israel to lose a battle to a much smaller opponent. It wasn't until God revealed the sin to Joshua that they were able to correct it. But, in the second battle with Ai, we see what the blinding affects of sin were upon this country, and you will experience the same blinding affects if you don't promptly deal with your sin.

First, sin takes your judgment away. Israel couldn't see sin twisting their judgment because they were so focused upon themselves. Sin affected their judgment because they were focused on their own strength. They thought they could conquer Ai without asking for God's help. Sin has a way of making us self-confident. We become very confident in what we can do. You will often find in your life that you will start planning things and doing things without even asking God for His help. This is one of the blinding affects of sin. All you have to do to see if sin is blinding you is look back and see how often you asked for God's help before you did anything. If you find yourself going straight into any project without asking for God's help, then sin has taken your judgment away.

Second, sin takes your strength away. It says in the verse above, *"Israel made as if they were beaten before them..."* Why did they do this? They did this because previously Ai chased them all the way back to their camp. A smaller opponent had victory over them. When you continually find yourself losing battles that you should have won, you need to stop and see if there is sin in your life. Sin has a way of making you weaker than the weakest. Don't ever take defeat for granted. Always take the time in defeat to look and see if sin has taken your strength away.

Third, sin takes your time away. Israel could have been fighting other battles, but sin took their time away by making them go back and fight a battle that they should have previously won. When you find that you never have enough time, that is a good indicator that sin could be affecting you. Sin keeps you from completing projects. Don't allow sin to steal your time. Keep your time productive by keeping away from sin.

Fourth, sin takes your victories away. Israel couldn't win as long as sin was in the camp. Sin will cause a person not to be as victorious as God wants. When you find yourself constantly losing battles, that is a good time to stop and find out why. Maybe sin has taken your victories away.

How can you avoid this? What should you do to keep sin from blinding you? Daily ask God to reveal sin and its affect on your life. I'm not talking about just repeating these words, but I am talking about truly asking God to show you when sin is in your life. You will find that God will show you sin if you deal with it immediately. Don't allow sin to have these blinding affects on your life. Keep yourself clean from sin, and you will find these things will not hinder you from victory.

Harmful Stubborn Ways

Judges 2:19

"And it came to pass, when the judge was dead, that they returned, and corrupted themselves more than their fathers, in following other gods to serve them, and to bow down unto them; they ceased not from their own doings, nor from their stubborn way."

Stubbornness isn't always a bad thing. I often teach my daughter that stubbornness can be good if you use it in a right manner. We ought to be stubborn concerning truth. We ought to be stubborn and oppose temptation. Stubbornness in itself is not bad if it is used properly.

On the other hand, stubbornness used improperly can be harmful. The children of Israel were very stubborn about doing wrong. God says, *"…they ceased not from their own doing, nor from their stubborn way."* God was willing to forgive and help Israel, but their stubbornness kept God from helping them and instead caused Him to judge them. Let me show you some of the harmful stubborn ways that caused God to judge them.

The first stubborn way is found Judges 17:6 when it says, *"In those days there was no king in Israel, but every man did that which was right in his own eyes."* These people determined their own righteousness. They didn't follow God's commandments, but they did what they felt was right. When you start justifying your own sin as good, that is very harmful to your spiritual well-being. Often we try to classify sin. We look at sin and say that one sin is worse than another. Friend, all sin is bad! I've yet to find a good sin in the Scriptures. You must be careful about being so stubborn about trying to justify your actions that you look at your sin and don't see it as wrong.

The second stubborn way is found in Judges 2:4 when it says, *"And it came to pass, when the angel of the LORD spake these words unto all the children of Israel, that the people lifted up their voice, and wept."* These people wept when they heard about their sin, but they never changed their ways. You can weep all you want to about how bad your sin is, but God is not as interested in a show as he is in action. I'm all for you being contrite about your sin, but move beyond the weeping and repent from your sin.

The third stubborn way is found in Judges 2:17 when it says, *"...they turned quickly out of the way which their fathers walked in..."* As soon as the man of God was dead, they quickly went back to doing wrong. Do you only do right in the presence of the preacher? Let me remind you that the preacher is not the one who will judge you, but God is the One Who judges. Don't be so stubborn about your sin that the only time you do right is when you are in the presence of God's servants.

The result of these stubborn ways is found in the verse above when it says, *"And it came to pass, when the judge was dead, that they returned, and corrupted themselves more..."* Christian, if you don't correct these stubborn ways, you will find yourself going deeper and deeper into sin. There is no stop to the level of depravity that your stubbornness will take you if you don't deal with it. I encourage you to be careful about having harmful-stubborn ways in your life. Instead of giving your sin a pass, deal with them and redirect your stubbornness to fight sin. This is the only way to turn harmful-stubborn ways into helpful-stubborn ways.

What Will You Do With Fear?

Judges 7:3

"Now therefore go to, proclaim in the ears of the people, saying, Whosoever is fearful and afraid, let him return and depart early from mount Gilead. And there returned of the people twenty and two thousand; and there remained ten thousand."

Whenever God commands you to do something, you will always find that fear will be something that you must overcome. When a person decides to step out by faith, two companions show up: fear and doubt. I've often said that fear is being afraid of that which has never happened. What you do with your fear will ultimately determine how much God uses you.

There are two stories in Judges that show me two completely different reactions to fear. The first story is found in the verse above when Gideon comes to the army of Israel and tells those who are afraid to go home. Amazingly, twenty-two thousand men went home. These men were afraid to face the great Midianite army, so instead of facing their fear they went home.

The other story is found in Judges 6:27 when Gideon was fearful of what the people would do if he tore down the images of Baal. The difference in this story is that Gideon did not listen to the voice of fear. He would not allow fear to stop him from doing what he was supposed to do. Though fear somewhat dictated his confidence, it did not stop him from obeying God by faith.

The results of these actions are two very different results. Because Gideon did not listen to fear and stepped out by faith and obeyed God, he not only became the leader of Israel, but he arguably was part of one of the greatest victories of all time. On the other hand, those twenty-two thousand men who went home could never say that they were part of that army who defeated the great Midianite army. Can you imagine the regret these men had as their children knew they could have been a part of that army?

These results were all dictated by how these people responded to fear.

When God wants you to do something, what do you do with your fear? When God commands you to witness to someone, do you listen to fear and stay quiet or do you obey God's voice and witness? When God commands you to give either to the church or to an individual, do you listen to fear and hold back or do you by faith give what God laid on your heart? There are many times throughout the week when God will tell you to do something, but fear will either cause you to withdraw and disobey or your faith will cause you to ignore the voice of fear and step out in obedience to God. The blessings of God upon your life will all be determined by what you do with fear.

Christian, certainly fear can paint a gruesome picture, but faith will always be rewarded. All you have to do is go back in your mind and remember the times when you ignored fear and obeyed God to see the positive results you obtained. I challenge you not to listen to fear. When fear begins to magnify its voice, always look to faith and obey. You will always find that the greatest victories are ahead when fear sounds its voice the loudest. Always ignore the voice of fear and you will find that great victories will follow. No, those victories will not be easy, but they will come.

Lessons from Defeat

Judges 20:21

"And the children of Benjamin came forth out of Gibeah, and destroyed down to the ground of the Israelites that day twenty and two thousand men."

Defeat should always be one of the hardest pills to swallow. If defeat doesn't bother you, that means you are not interested in what you're doing. Everyone faces defeat in their life, and what they learn from their defeat will determine their future.

The story from the verse above gives us several lessons from defeat that you should apply to your life. The children of Israel went to war against the tribe of Benjamin, and they lost. They had asked God whether to go, and God told them to go, but they still faced defeat. In this story you will find invaluable lessons that will encourage you when you face defeat.

First, defeat does not mean that you are wrong. God told the children of Israel to go to war against Benjamin and they still lost. They were not wrong in going to war even though they suffered defeat. If you suffer defeat in the midst of doing right, you must realize that does not mean that you are wrong. Too often we equate defeat with being wrong, and that can be the furthest from the truth. When you are fighting for truth, it can seem to be an uphill battle. In that battle, you will suffer defeat at different times, but that does not mean you are wrong. If you suffer defeat in the battle for truth, you are still right.

Second, defeat doesn't mean that you should quit. When Israel lost against Benjamin, they immediately went to God and asked Him if they should go up again against Benjamin, and God said to go again. God is teaching us that just because you suffered a defeat doesn't mean that you should quit. Many Christians don't have the stomach to continue on for the same cause in which they were just defeated. If you are fighting for truth, you must realize you cannot quit in the midst of defeat. Quitting in defeat will give the enemy the privilege of saying you were wrong. Don't give them that privilege! Keep on going though you have suffered a defeat.

Third, defeat **does mean** that you should continue doing right. These people kept praying, fasting and fighting though they had suffered defeat. Right does not become wrong when you suffer defeat. Right is always right, and you must continue to do right though you have experienced defeat. If you didn't reach a goal in your ministry, keep doing right. If you didn't see someone saved out soul winning, keep soul winning. If you failed to explain truth properly when teaching or preaching the Word of God, keep teaching and preaching the Word of God. Defeat should only be a setback and not the finish line.

Fourth, defeat **does mean** that you are one step closer to victory. Israel fought several battles before they eventually experienced victory. Every defeat meant that they were one step closer to victory. If you will keep getting up in your defeat, you will eventually experience victory. Be like the just man in Proverbs 24:16 who just kept getting up. Don't let defeat keep you down, for you are that much closer to victory.

Have you experienced a recent defeat? I certainly understand that defeat is not an easy pill to swallow, but you can take these lessons from defeat and let them encourage you to keep going. Don't let defeat defeat you. Keep going! Victory will come if you will keep getting up and doing right.

Wishing or Willing

1 Samuel 9:21

"And Saul answered and said, Am not I a Benjamite, of the smallest of the tribes of Israel? and my family the least of all the families of the tribe of Benjamin? wherefore then speakest thou so to me?"

My brother and I were recently in a conversation where he told me about a quote from a Louis L'amour book that said, "There are two kinds of people in this world, those who wish, and those who will. The world and its goods will belong to those who will." We discussed how our society is filled with people who wish they had things but never do anything about it, but that there are a few people who, in spite of background and obstacles, will their way into success.

Saul reminds me of the type of person who had a will to do something with his life. Israel desired for a king, and God told Samuel to go and anoint Saul to be king over Israel. When Samuel came and told Saul that God chose him to be king, Saul said, *"Am not I a Benjamite, of the smallest of the tribes of Israel? and my family the least of all the families of the tribe of Benjamin?"* Saul was acknowledging that his background was not the best, and that he did not grow up in a family with wealth. Yet, God still chose him to be king.

Saul is a great example to all that it doesn't matter what your background may be, if you have a will to do something with your life, then you can. It doesn't matter what your family may be like, you can always move past your family background and make something of your life if you have the will to do it. Your background and unfortunate situations in your life can either be an obstacle, or they can be opportunities that you will yourself above.

Friend, wishing that you could do something with your life will get you nowhere. This world is filled with people who wish they had something, and all they do is have their hand out waiting for the next giveaway. People who wish someone would give them an inheritance, or wish the government would come up with another program to make them wealthy will always stay in their miserable condition. Wishing has never moved one person out of their present condition.

The only thing that will cause you to rise above your background and condition is your will. If you have a will to do something with your life, you can rise above where you are and make something of it. I am not saying that you are going to become wealthy or popular, but what I am saying is that you can make something of your life.

When you look through the Scriptures, you will find that God used people who didn't wish, but they had a will to do something greater. They picked themselves up by their bootstraps and worked as hard as they could, and God helped them. The same can be said for today. God will help you if you have the will to start working your way up instead of using excuses for why you can't do anything with your life.

What are you going to do? Are you going to wish you could have a better life, or are you going to have the will to pull yourself out of where you are and do something with it. Yes, it always takes God's help, but God will not help until you will yourself to take the first step. God helped Job out of his miserable condition after he had the will to get up and take a step towards doing something.

God says in 2 Chronicles 16:9, *"For the eyes of the LORD run to and fro throughout the whole earth, to shew himself strong in the behalf of them whose heart is perfect toward him."* I challenge you today to stop wishing and start doing something about your situation. When you start doing something about it is when you will see God step in and show His power through your life.

Resting in the Goodness of God

Psalm 52:1

"Why boastest thou thyself in mischief, O mighty man? the goodness of God endureth continually."

What once seemed to be a promising life had become a life of exile. After the victory over Goliath, David must have thought that brighter days were ahead. He even knew that he was going to be king someday, but that time when he was anointed must have seemed a distant past.

In the writing of the psalm above, David was hiding in the land of Moab. Saul had just killed Ahimelech the priest and his family. Only Abiathar escaped to come and tell David what had happened. David knew that it was only a short time before Saul would find out where he was, and he knew Saul's intentions were to kill him. It was in these times when the only way David could receive comfort was from the goodness of God.

In times of lies, David rested in the goodness of God. Verse 2 says, *"Thy tongue deviseth mischiefs; like a sharp razor, working deceitfully."* David had been lied about to the nation of Israel. They were told that David had been disloyal. No matter where he went in Israel, they would report to Saul his whereabouts. The only thing in which David could receive comfort was the goodness of God. Likewise, when people lie about you, the one thing in which you must rest is the goodness of God. No one else may believe you, but you can be assured that the goodness of God knows the truth.

In times of attack, David rested in the goodness of God. David said, *"Why boastest thou thyself in mischief..."* Saul plotted how to kill David. David was under constant attack and was constantly fleeing to different places. No matter where he went, he found Saul's attack was present. When you have been lied about, and when the enemy attacks, you must rest in God's goodness to defend you.

In times of weakness, David rested in the goodness of God. David said he was going up against a *"mighty man."* He knew he was no match for Saul. So, the only place where he could find strength was in the goodness of God. He understood that God's goodness is what would strengthen him in his weakness.

What is God's goodness? God's goodness is a belief that God's integrity and righteousness sees the condition clearly. David knew that God understood the situation he was in and that God would reward Saul for what he was trying to do. David believed God's goodness would have mercy upon him, deliver him and justify his actions.

Friend, sometimes the only thing you will have to rest in is the goodness of God. Whenever you go through tough times as David did, you must realize that God's goodness will eventually justify you. When you are lied about, rest in the goodness of God that He will reveal the truth. When under attack, rest in the goodness of God that He will protect you. When you are weaker and have no way to truly overcome the attack of your enemy, rest in the goodness of God that He will give you the strength you need to face your battles. God's goodness will come through. Until you see God's goodness come through, do as David did in verse 9 and praise God.

Dealing with Grief in a Positive Manner

1 Samuel 30:6

"And David was greatly distressed; for the people spake of stoning him, because the soul of all the people was grieved, every man for his sons and for his daughters: but David encouraged himself in the LORD his God."

One of the most dangerous times in life for many people is when grief has stricken someone. In times of grief, many bad decisions have been made. In times of grief, many relationships have been damaged. In times of grief, many dreams have been quenched. If grief is dealt with in a positive manner, grief can be turned into victory.

David and his men found themselves in a time of grief. Some of the men who were with David did not deal with their grief in a positive manner. Had it not been for David doing the right thing, these men would have done some things that they most certainly would have regretted later. On the other hand, though David felt the same grief that his men felt, he dealt with it in a positive manner and it truly became the beginning of several victories in David's life. Let me show you how David dealt with grief in a positive manner.

First, he took time to grieve. His wives were gone, and he saw the grief of his men as many of them lost their wives and children. It says that David and the people with him wept. When grief comes your way, don't be afraid to cry. Crying during times of grief is like relieving the pressure from the pressure cooker. If you don't take time to grieve, you can become a walking time bomb that can hurt many people around you. There is nothing wrong with grieving. Jesus grieved when Lazarus was dead, and it is good for you to take time to grieve when going through times of grief.

Second, he didn't do or say something that he would regret. The men with him thought of stoning him, but instead of lashing out at them and reminding them how he took them in when nobody wanted them, he kept quiet and understood that they were reacting out of grief. Be careful when you are grieving that you don't add to your grief by doing or saying something foolish. Stay quiet and realize your feelings are raw at the moment.

Third, he took his grief to the LORD. The verse above says that David *"encouraged himself in the LORD his God."* Friend, this is the best thing you can do. Only the LORD can help you through your grief. He has been where you are, and He knows exactly how you feel. Crying on the shoulder of man will do nothing for you, but taking your grief to the LORD to receive encouragement will help. Likewise, encouraging yourself in the LORD also means that you allow the Scriptures to help you in your grief. Psalms is a good book to read during your time of grief.

Fourth, David got up and pursued. This is the most important step that you can take to get out of your grief. If you wallow in your grief it will never leave; however, if you get up and pursue life, you will find that you can overcome grief. The best pill for grief is to get up and continue to live. Continue to pursue life as if you had no grief. This is God's way of snapping you out of any self-pity that may keep you down.

Christian, how you handle grief will determine how many people you will be able to help. If David had stayed in the self-pity of grief, he would not have been able to take the throne of Israel. There is a throne that God wants you to sit upon, but you must get up from your grief and pursue life. It is then that God will take that grief and turn it into victory.

The Weakness of Strength

2 Samuel 3:30

"So Joab and Abishai his brother slew Abner, because he had slain their brother Asahel at Gibeon in the battle."

One of the amazing things about David's reign is the men who helped him. Joab was one of those men who I'm sure that David would have considered a right-hand man. Joab was involved in David's life from the beginning. The Scriptures do not make it clear whether David and Joab were friends in their childhood, but it would not surprise me if they were.

Joab was certainly a strength to David's reign. Joab was the man who led in the ascension to the throne of Israel. When the house of David and Saul were battling each other, it was Joab who led David's troops. It was Joab who was the general of David's troops through most of his life. Many of God's enemies were conquered because of Joab's strength to lead.

Yet, though Joab was a strong leader, he also had many weaknesses that at times were a hindrance to David. Very early in David's reign you will see the bitterness of Joab when his brother was slain by Abner. In an action of deceit, Joab slew Abner which weakened David's ascension to the throne. It was Joab who craftily brought Absalom back after he slew his half-brother.

Though Joab had many strengths, he also had many weaknesses. What I love about David is that he was able to overlook and overcome Joab's weaknesses by using his strengths for God's advantage. Instead of throwing away a man whom most would not have put up with, David found a way to let Joab's strengths be used.

Leaders should learn from David's example of using the strengths of individuals to further the cause of Christ. If a leader is not careful, they will not use anyone because they see the weakness of every follower. Great leaders are ones who learn how to take the strengths from an individual and use them for God's glory. It may take some creativity to find a way to use them, but leaders are supposed to be creative. As a leader you would be wise to find a way to use a person's strength in spite of their weaknesses because that is the only way they are going to grow.

Moreover, Christians need to learn to overlook the weaknesses of others and learn from their strengths. We live in a gossip society that loves to destroy leaders and people. It is not hard to find weaknesses in any person, for all people are sinners. Instead of spending your time focusing on the weaknesses of others, you would be wise to learn from their strengths. Don't let the weaknesses of individuals rob you from the lessons of their strengths. When you discover the weakness of someone, move on and continue to see their strengths.

Furthermore, every individual needs to be careful not to let their weakness keep them from using their strengths. We all know our own weaknesses. If we are not careful, we will allow our personal weakness to keep us from using the strengths we do have. Friend, you are not the only one who has a weakness. Yes, you should try to correct your weakness, but while you're working on correcting it don't let your strength go to waste. Take the strengths you do have and use them for the LORD.

Every strength has a weakness. You can either let the weakness rob you of the help and lessons that strength can give, or you can overlook the weakness and use the strength for God's glory. Don't let strength's weakness rob you from using it. As David found a way to use Joab in spite of his weakness, you need to find a way to learn from strength and let the strength help you to become a better Christian.

A Little Too Late

Psalm 51:2

"Wash me throughly from mine iniquity, and cleanse me from my sin."

It is easy to pass over the time frame from David's sin with Bathsheba to the time when the Prophet Nathan approached him. Close to a year had passed from the time when David committed adultery to the time his sin was revealed, and in that one year sin had taken a toll on David. This is why David said, *"Wash me throughly from mine iniquity, and cleanse me from my sin."* David knew the affect of sin on his life, and he wanted them completely removed.

What is more troubling to me is that after one year David saw sin's affect, yet many Christians have gone years in their sin. Imagine what sin has done to their lives. Just like cancer eats away at an individuals health, sin also eats away at the Christianity of many Christians. Psalm 51 shows us the affect that sin has on a Christian's life.

First, sin leaves a person guilt ridden. Verse 3 says, *"For I acknowledge my transgressions: and my sin is ever before me."* I truly believe one of the reasons many Christians do not have a good spirit is because they are carrying the guilt of sin. When Nathan approached David about the story of a man taking the lamb of a poor man, David's guilt got the best of him when he declared the penalty. A Christian cannot commit sin and guilt not take their heart. I seriously doubt the salvation of a person who commits sin and feels no guilt. Sin grieves the Holy Spirit, and because the Holy Spirit indwells the believer, His grieving will bring guilt upon the Christian.

Second, sin causes a person to make bad decisions. David said in verse 10, *"Create in me a clean heart..."* The heart is the source of all decisions. Proverbs 4:23 reminds us of this when it says,

"Keep thy heart with all diligence; for out of it are the issues of life." Sin always affects your decision-maker. This is why a person who sins often makes more bad decisions. Sin affected their heart; the source of their decisions.

Third, sin affects the spirit of a person. In verse 10, David acknowledged that his spirit had been affected. You will always find that a person's spirit is not what it used to be when they are in sin. People who once used to be patient will become short with others. People who once used to be loving will become hateful. It doesn't matter how hard you try to avoid it, sin always affects your spirit.

Fourth, sin robs your joy. David asked God to restore his joy. Christian, God wants you to live a joyful life, but sin will rob you of that joy. Sin will make the things of the Christian life seem like a prison sentence. It is always amazing watching people who get right with God begin to enjoy the things of God again. Sin's affect on your joy is tremendous, and you will never enjoy serving God as long as sin is in your life.

Finally, sin takes your security of freedom in Christ away. David begged God, *"uphold me with they free spirit."* What happened? Sin caused David to feel that God no longer loved him. Friend, that security you have in knowing that God loves you will be removed if you let sin reign in your life. This is why many people who are living in sin doubt their salvation. Sin took their security away.

We can never be reminded enough of the importance of quickly dealing with our sin. It is a little too late to avoid these affects of sin when you let sin roam free in your life. Deal with your sin immediately and you will find these affects will flee away. To the person who has allowed sin to reign in their life for a long time, God can still cleanse you and the affects of sin, but you must go to Him and confess them before He starts removing them from your life.

Absalom's Place

2 Samuel 18:18

"Now Absalom in his lifetime had taken and reared up for himself a pillar, which is in the king's dale: for he said, I have no son to keep my name in remembrance: and he called the pillar after his own name: and it is called unto this day, Absalom's place."

The name "Absalom" never brings positive thoughts to one's mind. Absalom was the son of King David. Here was a young man who had much potential, but many wrong attitudes and actions ruined that potential.

During the time when Absalom had thrust his father from the kingdom, he reared up a pillar so that all would remember him. It's sad that he thought a pillar would cause people to remember him in a pleasant light. Most likely Absalom knew in his heart that he had done wrong, and he wanted to be sure to turn that thinking around. So, he reared up a pillar and called it *"Absalom's place."*

That pillar certainly did become a memorial for Absalom, but not in a positive manner. Dr. Eremete Pierrotti, a French scientist, architect, and engineer, as an unsaved man journeyed through Palestine with the intention of disproving the Word of God. While visiting the heap of stones over Absalom's grave, an Arab woman came by with her little child, which she held by the hand. In passing, she threw a stone upon the heap marking the tomb of Absalom, and bade the child do the same. Dr. Pierrotti asked, "What do you do that for?" The Arab woman replied, "Because it was the grave of a wicked son who disobeyed his father." Dr. Pierrotti asked, "And who was he?" "The son of David," she replied. What Absalom tried to change he could not change, and that pillar which he erected still reminds people today of what he did.

Absalom's place reminds me of many things. First, Absalom's place reminds me of lost potential. Is there something in your life that is causing you to lose your potential? Absalom's pride was the thing that stole his potential, and it will steal yours. You must not allow a pillar of pride in your heart steal your potential as it did Absalom's.

Second, Absalom's place reminds me of vanity. Absalom was known for his long flowing hair. He was the pretty boy. Yes, I'm afraid we must be careful about allowing vanity to destroy us. Don't be so vain that you always have to have everything in place. If you are one who is always looking in a mirror, you have allowed Absalom's place of vanity to control your life. You are who you are, and trying to portray yourself to be something you are not is only hurting you. Be careful that you don't allow vanity to destroy you.

Third, Absalom's place reminds me of rebellion. This is no doubt what Absalom is remembered for the most. There was so much rebellion in his heart that he actually tried to have his own father killed so he could have the throne. Is there a part of rebellion in you? You should never pride yourself with having a little rebellion, *"For rebellion is as the sin of witchcraft."* (1 Samuel 15:23)

Do you find Absalom's place in your life? Friend, Absalom's place will destroy you. Just like the Arab woman knew what Absalom was about and taught her son to throw a stone upon his grave, you should also avoid having that pillar in your life. Don't the sins of pride, vanity, and rebellion destroy you. If you have let even a little of these things in your heart, remove them so that you will not be remembered as Absalom's place.

The Door of Death

Proverbs 5:8

"Remove thy way far from her, and come not nigh the door of her house:"

If I told you that behind a certain door was death, I would imagine you would do everything in your power to avoid that door. If death were behind a certain door, you would avoid it, set up danger signs around that door and warn every person not to get near that door. It would not matter how pretty the door would be for you would understand that death will occur if you open that door.

The father in the Book of Proverbs warns his son of such a door. He said in the verse above, *"...come not nigh the door of her house:"* This father was warning his son about the door of the strange woman. He warned his son that the door of the strange woman was dangerous. He said in verse 5, *"Her feet go down to death; her steps take hold on hell."* This father was warning his son that though the strange woman would try to lure him that he was to avoid going through the door to her house, because behind her door were the steps to death.

Friend, this warning is still true today. The door of the strange woman still leads to death. It is sad that we know this to be true, but many open that door only to find the death this father warned about. Though the warning of this door has been trumpeted for hundreds of years, many never learn the lesson and the danger of entering this door.

If the door of the strange woman is so deadly, then who is this strange woman? The word *"strange"* means foreigner. When God uses this word, he is warning us that any person who is not your spouse is strange. Of course, this was a father talking to his son, and that is why he used the phrase *"strange woman,"* but for the lady any man who is not her husband is a strange man. This "strange" person is not a person of the streets, but it is anyone to whom you are not married.

You must be very careful about how you conduct yourself with the opposite gender. Most people do not commit adultery or fornication with someone they do not know, but it is with someone they know that they commit these wicked sins. It is the person with whom you work or go to church of whom you must be careful. It is the person whom you call your friend of whom you must be careful. It is the person with whom you are closely associated of whom you must be careful. Always be polite and courteous to the opposite gender, but be careful to keep your distance.

The warnings God gives are grave. He says, *"her end is bitter as wormwood, sharp as a twoedged sword."* The bitterness this act will bring on your life is great. The pain it brings to you will be hard to heal. The honor you once had will be forever tarnished. The labors over which you toiled will all be in vain.

Friend, don't be the next casualty! Be careful with your interactions with the opposite gender. Certainly, you can interact, but don't cross the line and live a life of regret. God gives us the final warning of the door of death in the final two verses of this chapter when He says, *"His own iniquities shall take the wicked himself, and he shall be holden with the cords of his sins. He shall die without instruction; and in the greatness of his folly he shall go astray."* Don't be so foolish to think that you can handle the door of death. Avoid it with all of your being!

Walking in Integrity

Psalm 26:11

"But as for me, I will walk in mine integrity: redeem me, and be merciful unto me."

One of the most needed traits today is integrity. When you look at political leaders who say one thing on the campaign trail but do another thing once they are elected, you can see the need for integrity. When you see Christians who act and say one thing at church but are completely different when you see them out in the world, you can see the need for integrity. When you see our spiritual leaders say one thing from the pulpit but see their private life revealed in a negative manner, you can see the need for integrity.

Integrity is being honest and having strong moral principles in spite of what is going on around you. David said in the verse above, *"I will walk in mine integrity..."* When others around David did wrong, he did right. When others around him tried to get him to change, he did right and did not change. So, what does it mean to walk in integrity?

First, walking in integrity means doing right when you are all alone. David said in verse 2, *"Examine me, O LORD, and prove me; try my reins and my heart."* David understood that his private life was right. He knew what he thought when he was alone. He knew what he did when he was alone. That is why he told the LORD to examine him and prove him.

Would you want the LORD to examine what you do when you're alone? That is the measure of your integrity. Nobody may know your thought life, but you know it and so does God. It doesn't matter what facade you put on in front of others; it is what you do in private and what your thought life is like that is the true measure of your integrity.

Second, walking in integrity means doing right when you are attacked. Job 27:5 says, *"God forbid that I should justify you: till I die I will not remove mine integrity from me."* Job was under the attack of his friends, yet he would not change who he was. The measure of a person's integrity is how you respond to attack. When others do you wrong, integrity will continue to do right towards them. Integrity does not retaliate, rather it continues to treat the attackers as though they have not attacked. This is not easy, but this is the true measure of integrity.

Third, walking in integrity means to stand alone when others around you do not stand. Daniel 3:18 says, *"But if not, be it known unto thee, O king, that we will not serve thy gods, nor worship the golden image which thou hast set up."* This is the story of the three Hebrew children who were given another chance to bow down, but they would not bow even though everyone around them did and though they faced the fire of the furnace. The measure of one's integrity is truly defined when they must stand alone, and that stand will cost them everything. Too many people today have their finger to the wind trying to discern what the crowd is doing when they need to stand with the Scriptures. It doesn't matter what others do, the only thing that matters is doing right.

The benefit of walking in integrity is found in Psalm 41:12 that says, *"And as for me, thou upholds me in mine integrity, and wettest me before thy face for ever."* The benefit of walking in integrity is that it will carry you through all of these situations. It is what the LORD uses to help you through tough times.

Friend, let me encourage you to do right at all times. Don't let circumstances dictate your integrity, but do right when your attacked and alone. You may be the only one who stands, but you must realize that as you stand there is a God Who will stand with you. Your integrity is what brings you through your hard times. Be like Job who said, *"I will not remove mine integrity from me."*

Dealing with False Witnesses

Psalm 35:11

"False witnesses did rise up; they laid to my charge things that I knew not."

Everyone at some point in their life will be lied or gossiped about. It is never pleasant to be the subject of lies or gossip. Maybe you are going through a divorce and the lies being said about you are far from the truth. Maybe you are the recipient of church gossip that has assumed things about you that simply are not true. Maybe at the workplace someone said something about you that has put your job on the line. It really doesn't matter what the lies may be, they simply are not true and are destroying your name. Your first response is to retaliate and say things about the false witnesses that will expose them.

We don't know the story behind the psalm above, but one thing we do know is that David was dealing with people who were saying false things about him. When you read about David's life, you see that most of his life he truly tried to help people. Yes, he went through a small spell when he attacked others, but that was a very small portion of his life; however, his life was filled with instances when people falsely said things about him that just were not true. David shows us by example how to deal with false witnesses.

First, be friendly towards the false witnesses. Verse 14 says, *"I behaved myself as though he had been my friend or brother..."* Though these false witnesses were not David's friends, he treated them as if they were. This will be one of the hardest things to do. When I think of treating someone as a friend, there are several things I do for friends. I pray for friends. I am friendly with friends. I protect friends. These are just some of the things you would do for a friend. When you are dealing with false witnesses, pray for them, be friendly when you see them and don't ever allow false things to be said about them. When they are maligned, you need to tell the truth.

Second, tell God about your situation. In verse 17, David told God everything. Instead of whining to others about his situation, he told it to the One Who could handle it. Though you will be tempted to tell everyone about the attacks, the best way to handle them is to tell God what others are saying about you. God will take care of them if you will tell Him about it.

Third, act as if nothing happened. In verse 18, you see David in the temple thanking and praising God. He went on with his weekly schedule as if nothing happened. This is truly one of the most important things you can do. Don't change your weekly routines, but keep doing what you have always done. Don't come to church later, but keep going to church at the same time. Keep going to the same places you have always frequented, and don't avoid them just because you know they might be there. Staying in your routine will show that the lies are not going to change who you are and what you do.

Fourth, do right! In verse 24, David asked God to judge him. He could do this because he was doing right though others were not. Don't lower yourself to the character level of the false witnesses, but keep doing right. Your action of doing right in spite of the lies being thrown at you will eventually be the thing that vindicates you.

Friend, you can't deal with false witnesses. The only one who you can change is yourself. If you will take care of what you are supposed to do and do it right, God will take care of the lies being said about you and will publicly vindicate you. Wait on God, keep doing right and you will see the lies will eventually be exposed.

Mercy and Grace at Work

Psalm 103:8

"The LORD is merciful and gracious, slow to anger, and plenteous in mercy."

Two of the greatest attributes of God are mercy and grace. If God were not merciful and gracious towards us, we would be in a heap of trouble. It is only God's mercy that keeps us from burning in Hell, and it is His grace that offered us salvation. Yet, the mercy and grace of God does not stop at salvation. When studying Psalm 103, you see that mercy and grace are constantly at work in our lives. Let me show you how they work and how you can use them in your personal life with others.

First, mercy and grace cause God to be *"slow to anger."* Imagine how angry God would be with us if His mercy and grace didn't cause him to be *"slow to anger."* You need to be sure that you let mercy and grace help you not to be quickly angered with others. If married couples are going to keep their marriage strong with a happy atmosphere, then they need to let mercy and grace cause them to be slow to anger. Don't be quick to jump on your spouse when they do wrong. Parents, don't be so quick to be angry with your children. Pastors, be slow to anger with Christians who are not growing as fast as you would like. Leaders, let mercy and grace curb your anger when your followers do wrong. Every individual, no matter what category of life they fall in, needs to practice mercy and grace when others do them wrong.

Second, mercy and grace causes the punishment to end. Verse 9 says, *"He will not always chide: neither will he keep his anger for ever."* Aren't you glad that God ends the penalty when we do wrong? Likewise, you need to be sure to end the penalty with others when they do wrong. It is not good to continually hold something over the head of someone when they have done wrong. The penalty has to end at some point. To continually punish someone because they did something five or ten years ago is simply not allowing mercy and grace to work. Let the punishment end! Stop holding a grudge against someone because of what they did in the past. Move on and let mercy and grace work in your life.

Third, mercy and grace doesn't deal with people according to their sins. Verse 10 shows us that God deals with us according to His grace and mercy and not according to our sins. Friend, apply mercy and grace to the individual who has done wrong. In other words, don't always mistrust someone just because they did wrong. Let your mental attitude towards people be one that you deal with them as if they had never done wrong.

Fourth, mercy and grace allow people to have a bad day. Verse 14 says, *"For he knoweth our frame; he remembereth that we are dust."* This is so important to the health of any relationship. You must give people a chance to have a bad day. Don't be quick to judge and punish someone because they did one thing wrong. Let mercy and grace govern your emotions and help you not to be cross with others all the time. Realize they are human, and humans will have a bad day.

I am not condoning sin, neither am I saying that we should sweep sin under the carpet. I am saying that we need to be merciful and gracious to others so they have a chance to grow. It is the mercy and grace of God that gives us the opportunity to grow. You will never see others grow into a better person without letting mercy and grace work. As you go throughout your day, let mercy and grace govern how you deal with those who make a mistake.

Something's Wrong

1 Kings 1:26

"But me, even me thy servant, and Zadok the priest, and Benaiah the son of Jehoiada, and thy servant Solomon, hath he not called."

When Adonijah presumptuously took the throne of Israel while David was still alive, it is astonishing to see how the people foolishly followed him. It is sad that though David was alive, Adonijah had a philosophy that his dad was too old to really lead and that he had better ideas for Israel. Beyond that fact, there were some definite symptoms that something was wrong. These symptoms should have been seen by all of Israel, but they blindly followed this foolish young man to the detriment of some. Let me show you the symptoms they should have seen.

First, he avoided the preacher. Adonijah didn't call Nathan the prophet, instead he avoided him for he knew his actions were wrong. You can always tell when someone is wrong because they avoid the preacher. It is not that the preacher is anyone of himself, but it is Whom he represents that makes him special. When a young person doesn't want to be around the preacher, you can be assured that something is wrong. When a Christian avoids the preacher, you can be confident that something is wrong. If you are doing right, you will have no problem being around the preacher, but when you are not doing right you won't want anything to do with him.

Second, he avoided the spiritual leaders. Adonijah not only avoided Nathan the prophet, but he also avoided Zadok the priest. Zadok would have been a positive spiritual influence in his life, but he avoided him. This should have alerted Israel that something was wrong because he avoided the spiritual leaders in his life. When someone wants nothing to do with the spiritual leaders whom God has placed in their life, then something's wrong. When you avoid your Sunday school teacher, church staff leaders and spiritual leaders who have influenced you in the past, something is wrong. If you are doing right, you will want those spiritual leaders involved in your life.

Third, he avoided his family. It is interesting that Adonijah did not tell his father David what he was doing, neither did he invite Solomon or any other family members because he knew he was wrong. When a person shuts out their family, there is something definitely wrong. Parents should always be alerted when their child is avoiding them and other family members. Someone is turning their heart away from family. When a person is right with God they will not avoid their family, rather they will be drawn closer to them.

Fourth, he avoided his parent's influences. Adonijah didn't want Benaiah to be a part of his kingdom. Benaiah was in charge of David's guards. In other words, he would have been an advisor to the king. When a person avoids the positive influences from the past who influenced their parents and spiritual leaders, something is wrong. It is always a definite sign that something is wrong when someone criticizes the methods and men of God from the past.

You must be wary of individuals who have these four symptoms in their lives. People who avoid these influences will be a negative influence in your life. Avoid these people and have nothing to do with them. These four influences are important to anyone's life and should never be avoided if you want God to bless you. Be sure that in your own life you are not avoiding these influences. Let these four areas constantly influence you for right.

Living on Your Own

Proverbs 4:12

"When thou goest, thy steps shall not be straitened; and when thou runnest, thou shalt not stumble."

In Proverbs 4, Solomon is preparing his son to go live on his own. He reminded his son that his father also taught him the same things. He said in verses 3-4, *"For I was my father's son, tender and only beloved in the sight of my mother. He taught me also..."* Solomon stressed the importance of his son taking the same things his father taught him to let them guide him when he was on his own.

First, Solomon said, *"retain my words."* He was begging his son not to let what he taught him go in one ear and right out the other. Every person needs to heed this advice. Your parents taught you how to make it in life, and their advice to you was to keep you from ruining your life. Many young people ruin their lives because they think they know more than their parents. So, they live in such a manner as to prove their parents wrong. You must understand that your parents truly want the best for you, and their counsels to you should be retained and followed.

Second, Solomon said to *"keep my commandments."* In other words, he was telling his son not to abandon the rules under which he lived in his father's house. Often young people think they have the freedom to live any way they want when they leave their parent's home, and they do; however, those rules their parents had for them were there to protect them from ruining their lives. It would be wise for every person to remember the rules by which they lived growing up and live by those same rules. Having a personal curfew will keep the single person from ruining their life in sin. Avoiding the wrong places and friends will keep them from being associated with wrong. Staying involved in church will help the single person to continue to keep their life on track for God without having to trudge through heartache.

Third, Solomon taught his son to keep gathering wisdom after he left home. He said in verse 7, *"Wisdom is the principal thing; therefore get wisdom..."* A young person should continue to learn once they leave home. They should learn the things that will help them live for God. Just because a person has graduated from high school and college doesn't mean they should stop learning. Life should be a continual classroom of gathering wisdom to help in life.

Fourth, Solomon reminded his son not to forget the examples he taught him. He said, *"I have taught thee in the way of wisdom..."* Solomon reminded his son that he didn't just give him information, but he showed him how to live by example. Let me encourage every young person to avoid the mentality that your parent's lifestyle is out-of-date. If you have parents who lived what they taught, you are privileged to learn first hand what to do and what not to do in life.

Solomon said in the verse above, *"When thou goest..."* Every person will eventually live on their own. Solomon warned that the reason they need to heed these warnings is because *"thy step shall not be straightened."* In other words, your parents won't be there to correct you and save you from heartache once you get on your own. This is why it's imperative to absorb everything your parents teach you and live by it so their wisdom will be the correcting agent in your life when you are on your own. Always remember that mom and dad are not always going to be there to stop you from wrong.

It's time every young person pays close attention to their parent's instruction because they will eventually be living on their own. If young people don't pay close attention to their parent's instruction, they will miss something that is going to help them in life. Every young person needs to give their life to paying attention to their parent's advice and teachings. Those teachings and advice are there to help you enjoy life. Don't ignore them!

The End of the Story

Proverbs 23:18

"For surely there is an end; and thine expectation shall not be cut off."

There are laws that cannot be broken no matter how hard you try to break them. For instance, what goes up must come down. Wherever there is sin there is death. One of the laws that many tend to overlook is that when there is a beginning there is always going to be an end. You may like the beginning, but you better be sure that the end is as good as the beginning.

God warns us in the verse above, *"For surely there is an end..."* God is warning us that there is an end to sin. He says in the previous verse, *"Let not thine heart envy sinners..."* You may always see the pleasure that sin advertises, but there is also an end to that sin. Sin will never advertise its end. The only thing that sin can advertise is how it starts out. It can advertise the fun of a dance floor. It can advertise the pleasure of a night of sin. It can advertise the camaraderie of a night out with the boys at the bar. It can advertise these things for there is pleasure in them.

What sin cannot do is advertise the end of these things. It cannot adversities the end of the STD's a person gets from living a promiscuous lifestyle. It cannot advertise the end of an Al Capone who had any lady he wanted, but syphilis ate his brain to the point that he had the mind of a 12 year-old when he died. Sin doesn't advertise that! Sin cannot advertise the young lady having to rear a child by herself because she got pregnant out of wedlock. Sin cannot advertise the prisoner sitting in his cell because of an action he performed while drunk or under the influence of drugs. No, sin cannot advertise the end, because the end of sin cannot sell.

You cannot sell a person working two and three jobs to get themselves out of debt from a life of credit card spending. You cannot sell cirrhosis of the liver from a person who pickled their liver from a life of alcohol. You cannot sell emphysema from a person who has smoked all their life. You cannot sell the broken marriages from a one night stand that no one would ever find out about. You cannot sell the broken family that was caused because someone dropped out of church over a disagreement. Sin cannot sell these things and more.

Friend, wherever there is a beginning there is always going to be an end. Instead of being enamored with the beginning of something, you would be wise to invest time in looking at the end before you ever partake of something. The end is where you are going to end up. So, before you ever decide to take sin's advertisement, you had better do research on the end and see what sin brings.

On the other hand, God can sell His ending because His lifestyle brings joy and satisfaction. No, the beginning of the Christian life is not always going to sell, but the end of the Christian life is always one of satisfaction. The Christian who has served God their entire life will never regret living that life. Friend, you may wonder if you are doing the right thing in serving the LORD, but you must remember there is an end. Don't envy the way of the sinner, for the end of their way is death. Keep your eyes on the LORD, for the end of His way is satisfaction.

Wisdom From the Successful

Proverbs 30:24

"There be four things which are little upon the earth, but they are exceeding wise:"

The greatest place to gain wisdom is from those who have been successful. When I was a youth, I often had the opportunity to sit down with successful men of God and ask them questions. I watched what they did and copied the areas of their success because I wanted to be successful in the ministry.

In the verse above, God gives us insight from creation. He says that there are four things that are *"exceeding wise."* God uses four little creatures to teach us wisdom on how to be successful. The lessons from these four little creatures are invaluable to anyone who wants to be successful in their life.

First, preparation is important to success. Verse 25 says, *"The ants are a people not strong, yet they prepare their meat in the summer;"* The ant understands that its livelihood depends on preparing in the summer. The summer is a time of plenty. Yet, the ant understands that plenteous times will not always be there if they don't prepare.

The degree of your success highly depends upon how well you prepare. Last minute preparation always leads to failure. You may be able to succeed for awhile on last minute preparation, but eventually it will kill you. Those who are successful prepare well in advance. Planning takes away most of the stress in any project. Financially you need to plan ahead if you are going to be financially stable. In business and church matters you must prepare ahead to succeed. Those who are successful are those who prepare.

Second, reality is important to success. Verse 26 says, *"The conies are but a feeble folk, yet make they their houses in the rocks;"* The cony is wise enough to know its own weakness.

Successful people learn their weaknesses and surround themselves with people who are stronger than they are in their weak areas. To lie to yourself about your weakness is only hurting yourself. Know your weakness, and let others who are stronger in those areas help you.

Third, teamwork is important to success. Verse 27 says, *"The locusts have no king, yet go they forth all of them by bands;"* The locusts are strong because they work together. You will never succeed on your own. It takes teamwork to succeed. If you are a leader and you try to do everything by yourself, you will never reach your potential. Your potential is determined by your preparation and your delegation. If you can't learn to let your team do some work, you will limit your success. Always remember that teamwork will produce the greatest success.

Fourth, work is important to success. Verse 28 says, *"The spider taketh hold with her hands, and is in kings' palaces."* Nobody will ever succeed without hard work. The spider didn't look for a handout; instead, the spider took *"hold with her hands"* to get into the palace. Stop looking for an easier way and just work. You may not be as smart and talented as everyone else, but you can always outwork the rest and still be successful. It is normally those who work the hardest who see the greatest success.

You will never be successful without these four things in your life. I challenge you to keep these four things in front of you at all times as reminders of what it takes to be successful. Success is not a secret, but it is a result of preparation, reality, teamwork and work. You will never succeed without implementing all four of these things in your life.